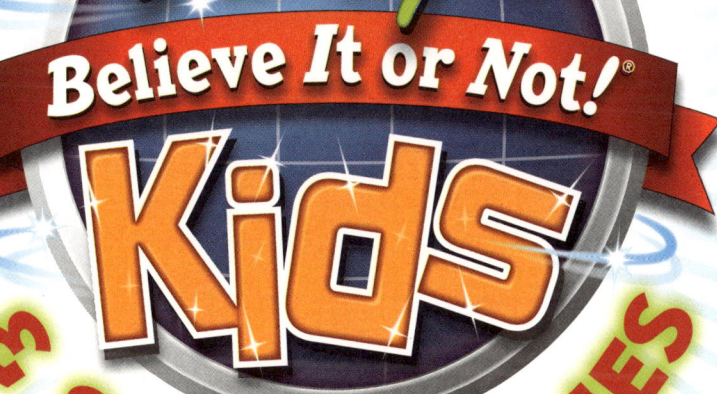

FUN FACTS
Ripley's Believe It or Not!® Kids
& SILLY STORIES

Ripley PUBLISHING

Consultant Camilla de la Bedoyere
Design Rocket Design
Reprographics Juice Creative

Published by Ripley Publishing 2013
Ripley Publishing, Suite 188, 7576 Kingspointe Parkway,
Orlando, Florida 32189, USA

10 9 8 7 6 5

Copyright © 2012 by Ripley Entertainment, Inc.
Reprinted 2012, 2013 (twice), 2014
All rights reserved. Ripley's, Believe It or Not!, and
Ripley's Believe It or Not! are registered trademarks
of Ripley Entertainment Inc.

ISBN 978-1-60991-054-9 (US)

Library of Congress Cataloging-in-Publication Data

Fun facts and silly stories.
       p. cm. -- (Ripley's believe it or not!)
    ISBN 978-1-60991-054-9
 1. Curiosities and wonders--Juvenile literature.
    AG243.F855 2012
    031.02--dc23
                                    2012024617

Manufactured in China
in June/2014
5th printing

WARNING
Some of the stunts and activities in this book are
undertaken by experts and should not be attempted
by anyone without adequate training and supervision.

First published in Great Britain in 2013 by
Young Arrow, Random House,
20 Vauxhall Bridge Road, London SW1V 2SA

www.randomhouse.co.uk

Addresses for companies within The Random House
Group Limited can be found at
www.randomhouse.co.uk/offices/htm

The Random House Group Limited Reg. No. 954009

A CIP catalogue record for this book is available from
the British Library

ISBN 9780099568049 (UK)

No part of this publication may be reproduced in whole
or in part, or stored in a retrieval system, or transmitted
in any form or by any means, electronic, mechanical,
photocopying, recording, or otherwise, without written
permission from the publisher.

For information regarding permission, write to VP
Intellectual Property, Ripley Entertainment Inc., Suite 188,
7576 Kingspointe Parkway, Orlando, Florida 32819
Email: publishing@ripleys.com
www.ripleybooks.com

PUBLISHER'S NOTE
While every effort has been made to verify the accuracy
of the entries in this book, the Publishers cannot be held
responsible for any errors contained in the work. They
would be glad to receive any information from readers.

FUN FACTS

Ripley's Believe It or Not! Kids

& SILLY STORIES

1

Question:
When is a sardine not a sardine?

Answer:
When it gets together with thousands of friends to make a giant dolphin!

This huge school of sardines in the shape of a dolphin was snapped by a photographer in the Philippines. It is made up of thousands of sardines that group together for protection from predators.

A slug has no nose.

How does it smell?

Terrible!

A BOX JELLYFISH HAS ENOUGH VENOM TO KILL 50 PEOPLE.

CROCS EAT ROCKS!

A bellyful of stones helps them digest food and stay underwater.

Turtles can breathe through their butts

Although turtles breathe using their lungs like most animals, they also have a pair of sacs in their butt that take in water and extract oxygen from it. So, they really can "breathe through their butts".

Look guys, pretty bubbles!

horses do not vomit

WANT TO KNOW WHY? Horses have a very strong muscle at the top of their stomach that closes after food is swallowed. It acts as a one-way route that lets food go down, but not come back up again.

KANGAROOS
don't move backward.

They can only jump, not walk!

A poison dart frog has enough poison to kill **10** people.

Dogs sweat through their feet—most of their sweat glands are on their paw pads.

can COWS climb ladders?

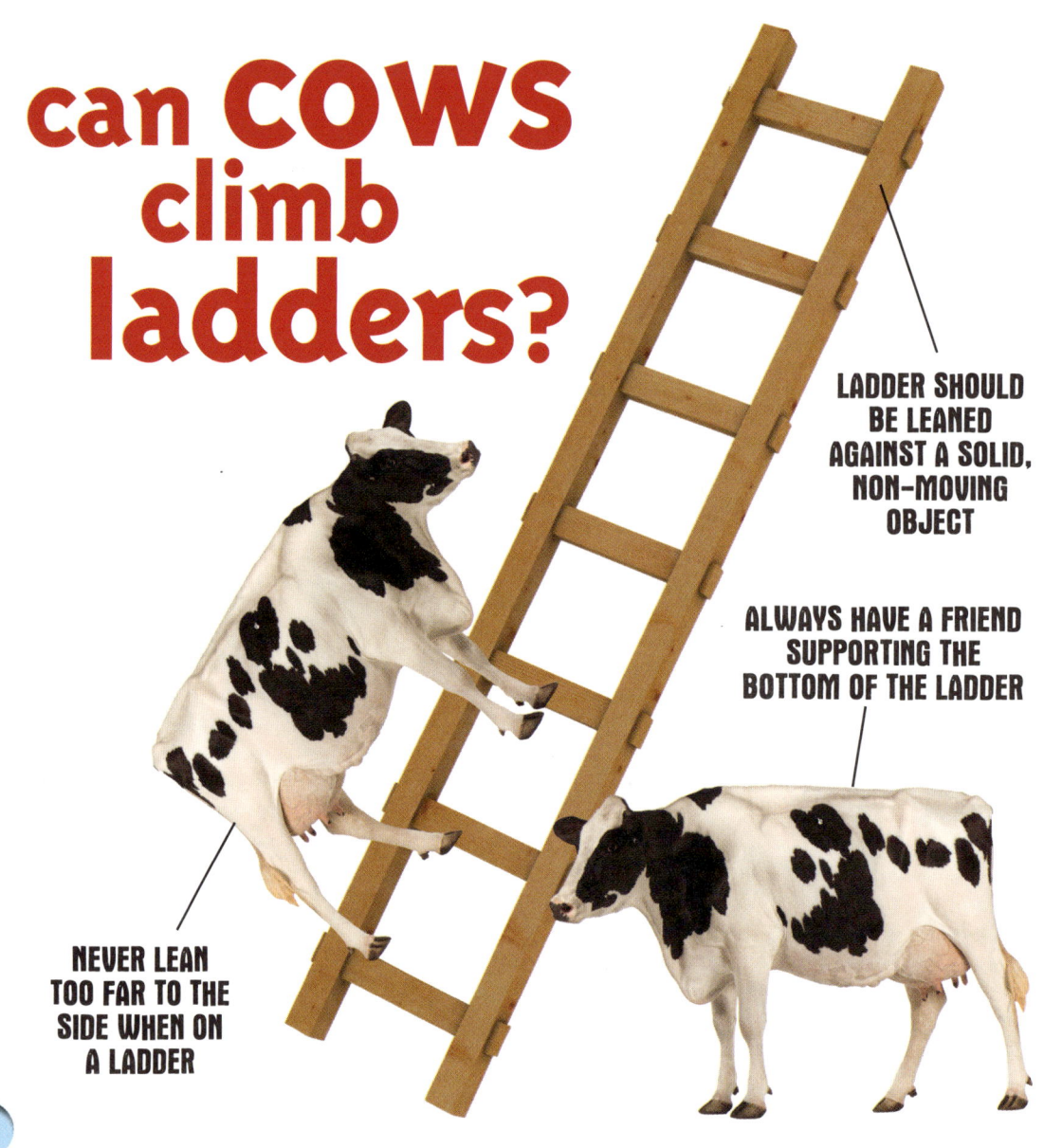

LADDER SHOULD BE LEANED AGAINST A SOLID, NON-MOVING OBJECT

ALWAYS HAVE A FRIEND SUPPORTING THE BOTTOM OF THE LADDER

NEVER LEAN TOO FAR TO THE SIDE WHEN ON A LADDER

Believe it or not, this poor creature got his head stuck between the rungs of a ladder! An animal inspector managed to free him and return him safely to his herd.

OTHER COWS NOT HELPING

After eating, a fly vomits its meal up, and then **eats it again!**

NO WEIGH!

Milly is quite possibly the smallest dog in the world. She stopped growing at three months, and weighs just under 6 ounces (170 g).

Chihuahuas usually reach a height of 6 to 10 inches (15 to 25 cm) but Milly measures just 2½ inches (6.5 cm) tall.

It's a Dog-Lion-Zebra

Dog grooming is taken to the extreme in some contests in the U.S.A. The pampered pets are clipped, brushed, and dyed to look like other creatures or even movie characters. Some have been transformed to look like horses, lions, zebras, pandas, or a mix of animals.

Cheeky zebra sneaking up behind!

"I feel silly!"

Lion's mane

Long fake tail

17

Lobsters have blue BLOOD.

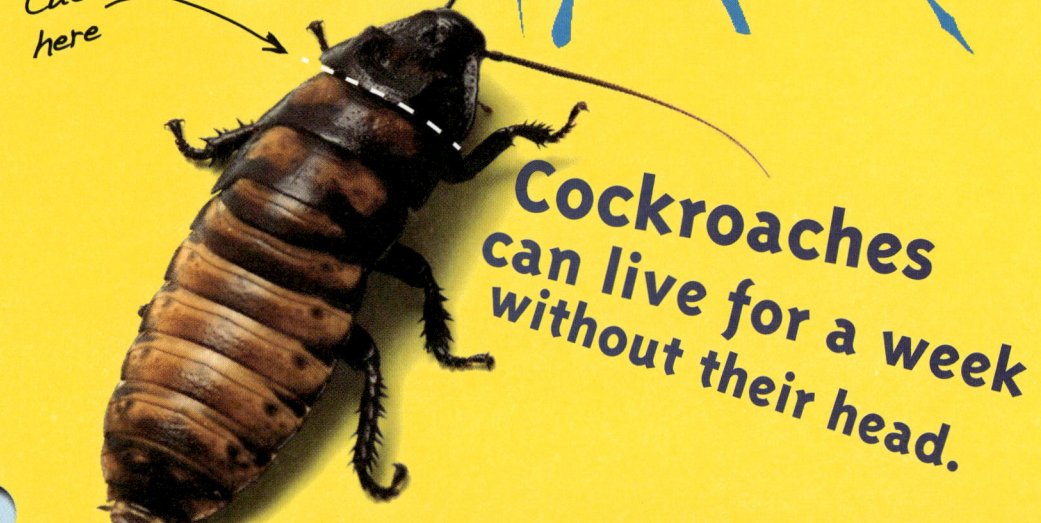

Cut here

Cockroaches can live for a week without their head.

More people are **TRAMPLED** to death by cows than are killed by sharks.

Earthworms have FIVE hearts.

The heart of a blue whale is the size of a small car.

It beats nine times a minute. A human heart beats around 70 times a minute.

PYGMY HIPPO POO CAN FLY!

The animals swirl their tail around when they poo. This flings the poo around to mark their territory.

THE WOOLLY

BEFORE

Shrek the sheep hid in caves in New Zealand for six years so by the time his coat was eventually cut it weighed 60 pounds (27 kg)!

MAMMOTH

AFTER

A snail produces such a thick layer of slime that it could crawl over a **razor blade** without damaging itself.

A RAT CAN GNAW THROUGH ALMOST ANYTHING.

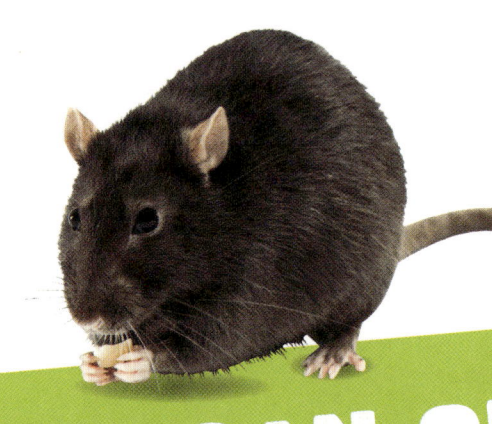

They cause a quarter of electric cable breaks and nearly as many problems with phone lines.

Rats eat or spoil around **ONE FIFTH** of the world's food every year.

Hello? Where am I?

26

Believe it or not, goats can climb trees! They climb up argan trees, found mostly in Morocco, because they like to eat the fruit, which is similar to an olive.

must be kidding!

Help!

A hippo can yawn wide enough for an eight-year-old to stand in its mouth!

Some sharks **walk** on their fins underwater.

A sailfish can leap through the air at 68 mph. (109 km/h)

Elephants produce around **200 pounds** (90 kg) of poo every day.

Heads up!

The peacock mantis shrimp has front legs strong enough to smash BULLETPROOF GLASS!

HOPPING MAD

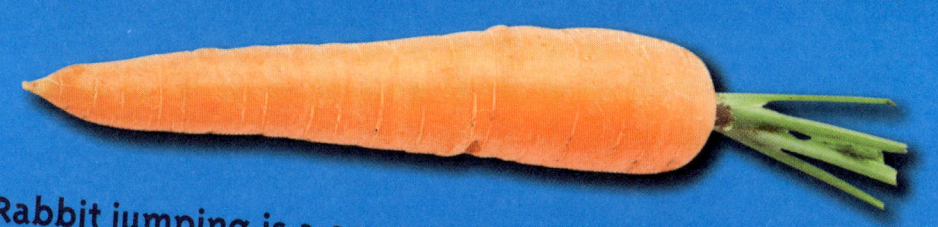

Rabbit jumping is a crazy new sport that began in Scandinavia and can now be found all around the world. The ideal jumping rabbit has long legs and a long back. Champions can clear fences that are over 3 feet high (1 m), and can jump up to 10 feet (3 m) in the long-jump competition.

concentrate!

legs tucked well in

awesome "big air"

Check out one of my classic "text book" jumps... Look and learn!

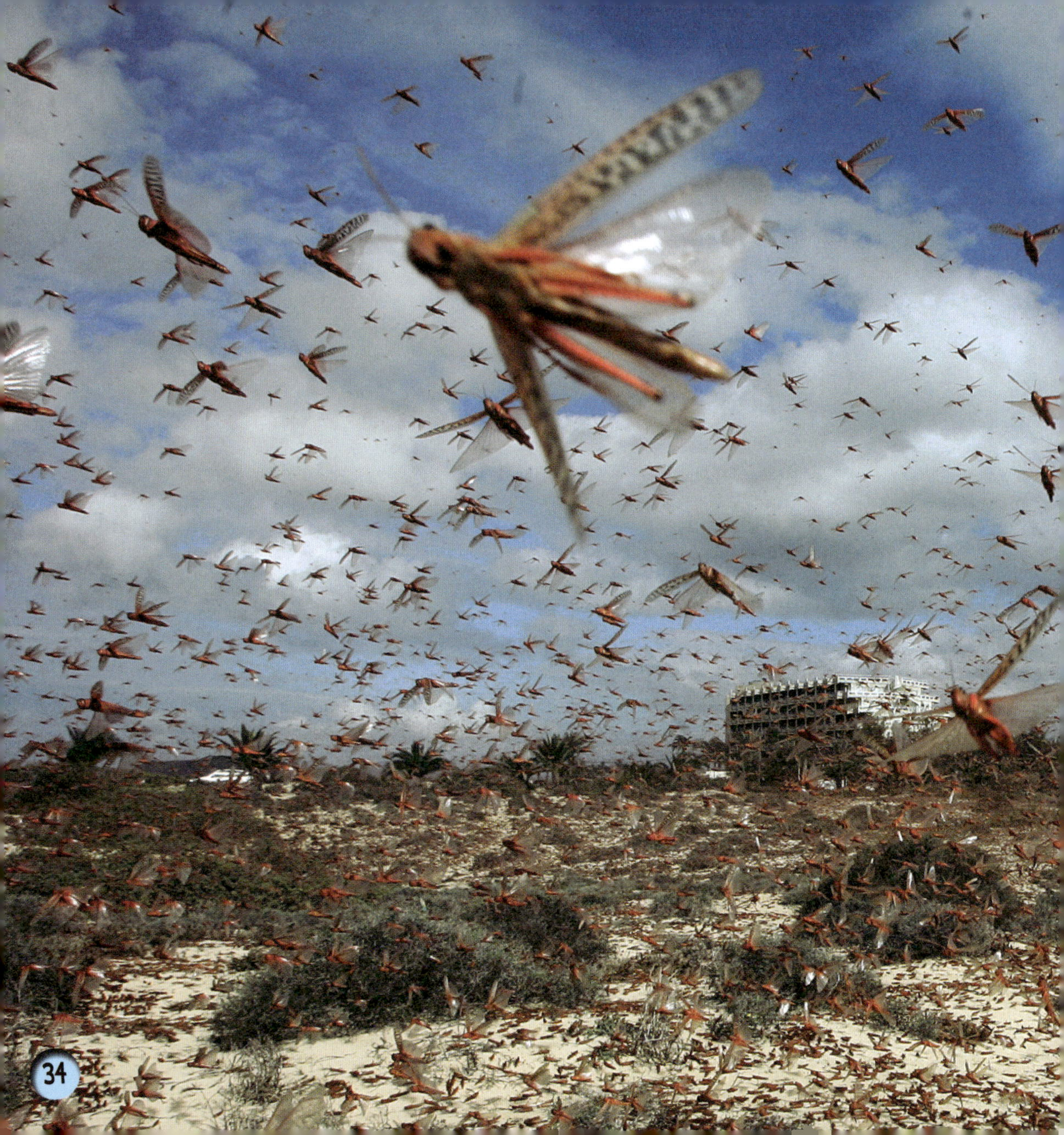

1,000,000 locusts make a swarm!

STARFISH CAN REGROW LOST ARMS

Sometimes a whole new starfish will grow from just one severed arm and part of the central body!

Spiders' brains are so **LARGE** that they run all the way down into their legs.

LUCKY DUCKY

Lucky the duckling can walk again after being fitted with a duck shoe! The specially made sandal helped her leg to heal after she broke it.

BOING!

Scarlett, a piglet from England, just loves the trampoline! The piglet's secret skill was discovered when her owners put her on their daughters' trampoline.

Daddy, is it my turn yet?

Brrrr!

These swallows in Canada are keeping each other warm in a snowstorm. They fluff up their feathers and huddle together to share body heat.

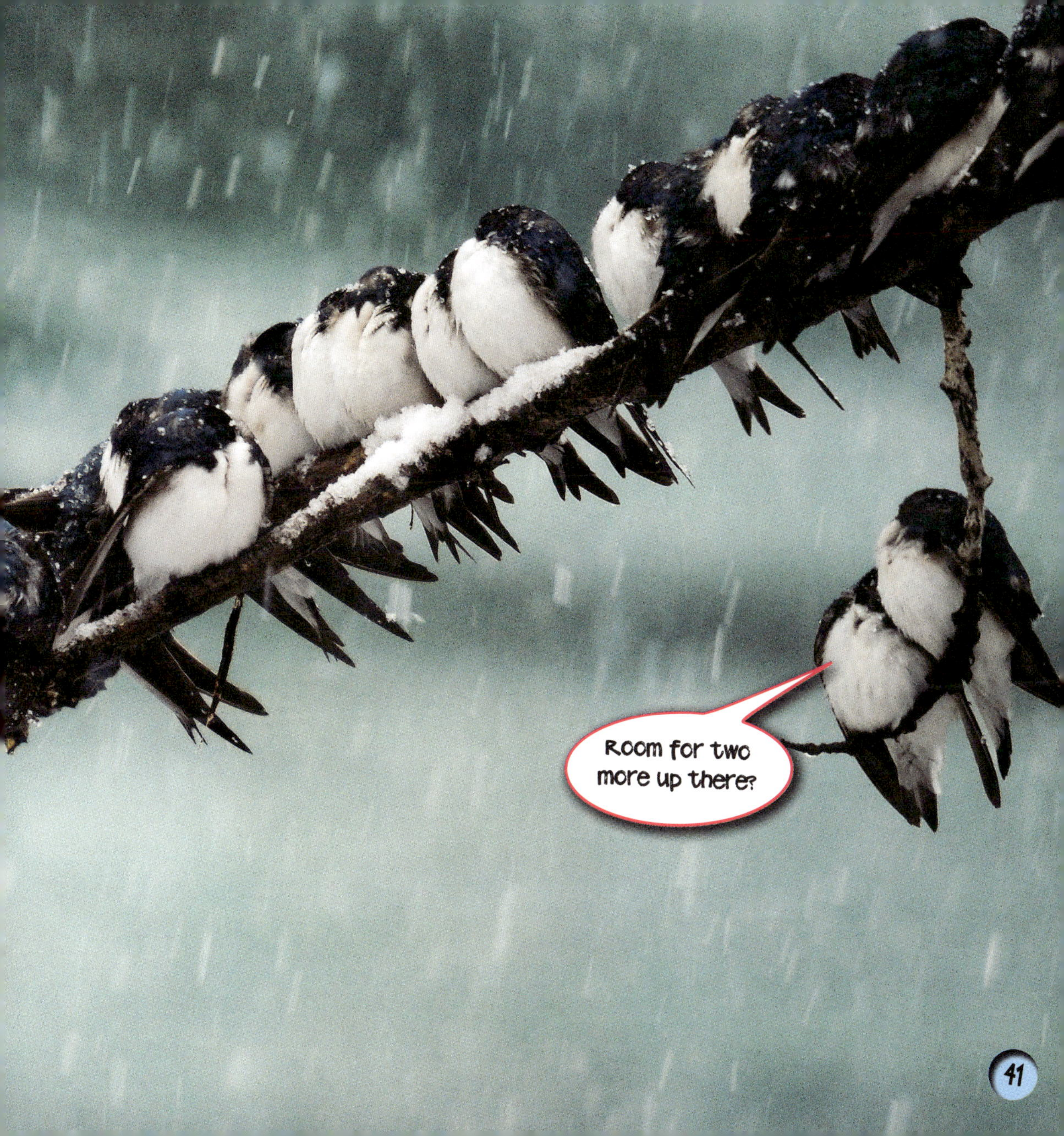
Room for two more up there?

actual size!

THE AMERICAN BULLFROG TADPOLE CAN MEASURE 6.75 INCHES LONG!
(17.2 cm)

your "regular" tadpole

The call of an American bullfrog is so low it sounds like the mooing of a cow!

Some jellyfish eat their own babies.

Cows, dogs, and birds can have different accents, depending on where they live.

Fish scales are used to make lipstick shimmer.

Pucker up!

COOL CHICKS

Oooh, check him out girls!

These chickens were almost bald when they were rescued from factory farms in England. Animal welfare officers kept them warm by dressing them in these bright sweaters, or "chickinis".

Alright darling?

cock-a-doodle ladies!

Newborn Galapagos tortoises are 3,000 times smaller than their mothers!

565 pounds
(256 kg)

3 ounces
(87 g)

This little guy will take 30 years to get to the same size as its mother.

WOMBAT POO COMES OUT IN CUBES.

SPARE PARTS

The glass lizard has no legs and sometimes no tail! If the lizard is attacked, its tail breaks off and wriggles away to trick the attacker.

Dogs pant up to 300 times a minute.

Phew, it's hot in here!

SUCK-E-E-R-R

This is so boring! Where's my Xbox?

52

Scientists gave 25 octopuses Rubik's Cubes to play with to see which tentacle they liked to use to pick things up.

SCIENTISTS think THAT...

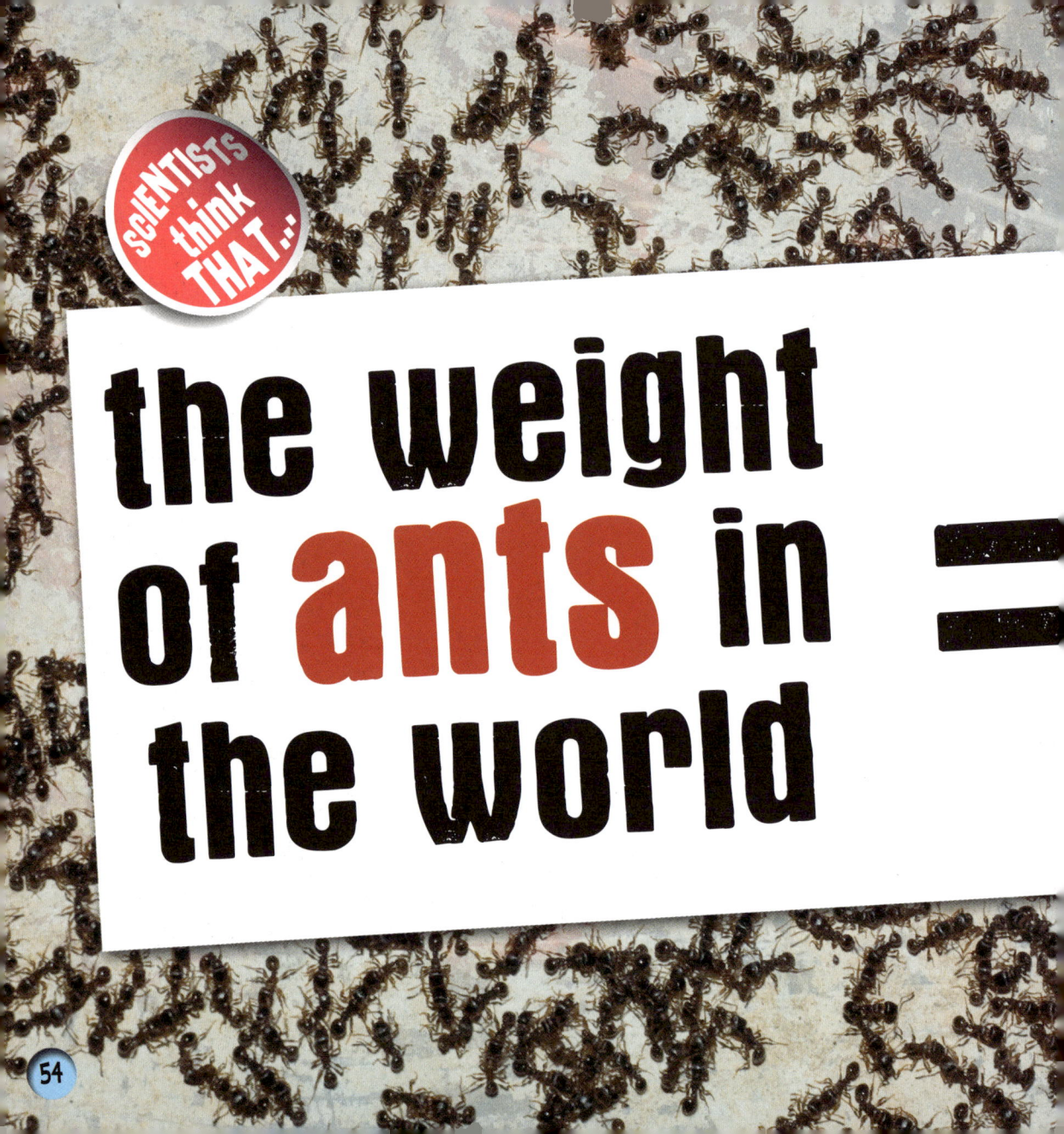

the weight of **ants** in the world =

the weight of people in the world

SQUEEZE!

Ksyusha the kitten can climb in and out of some tight places including this jar! She started climbing into jars when she was a few weeks old, and now hides in all sorts of places, including the washing machine!

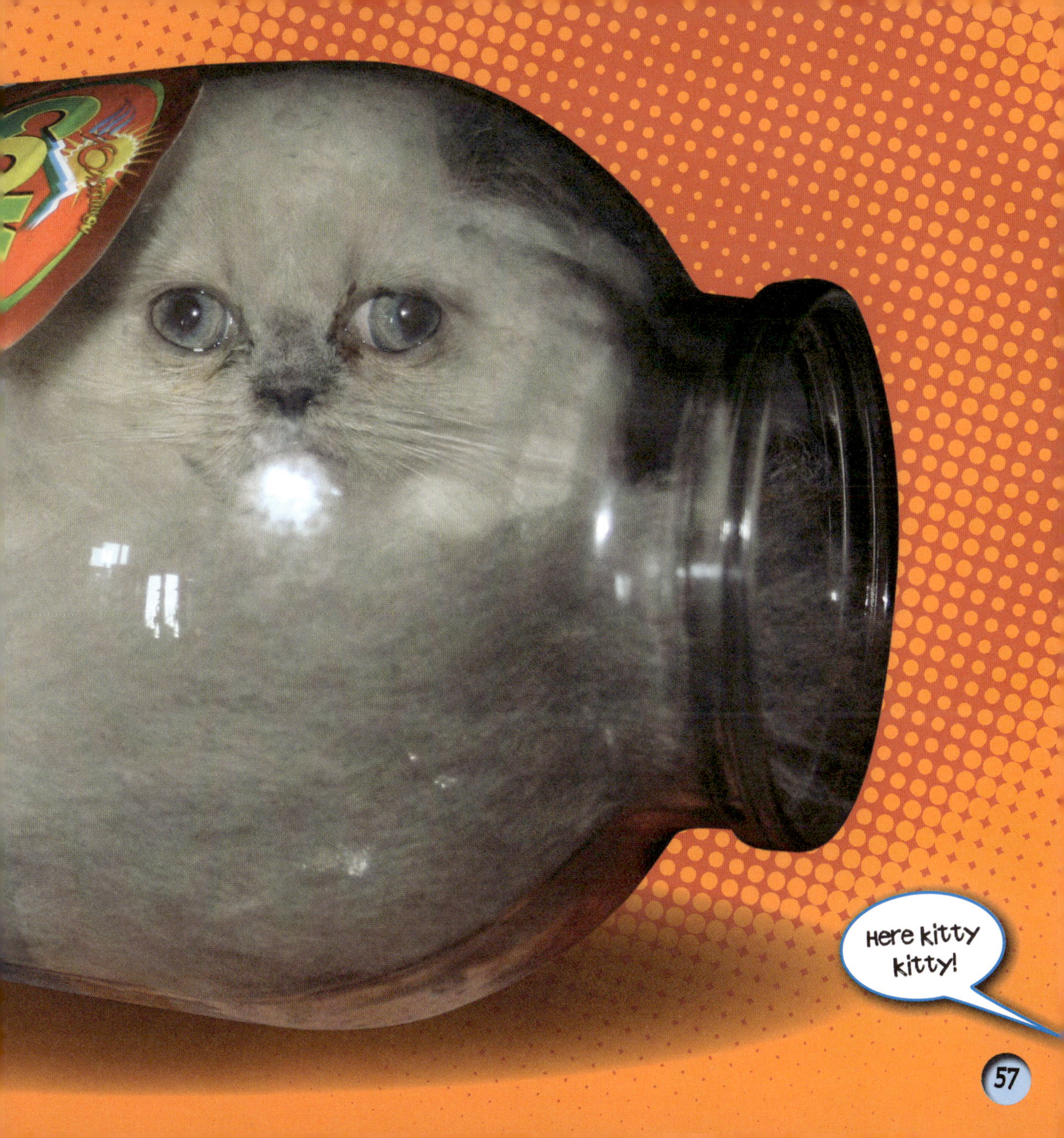
Here kitty kitty!

THORNY BUGS

Believe it or not, these spiky looking thorns are actually female thorn bugs feeding on a tree branch. Great camouflage!

A gecko can hang from a ceiling with just ONE toe.

An octopus has **THREE** hearts.

Cuttlefish can change their patterns many times **every second.**

Baa baa red sheep, have you any wool?

SEEING RED

This flock was painted red to cheer up people driving past a farmer's field in Scotland! Sometimes farmers dye their sheep to help count them, or to stop them from being stolen.

Who's a pretty boy then?

Me?

Whipper the budgie is not like other budgies. He suffers from "feather duster" disease, which means he grows extra long feathers that fluff up like a feather duster!

SHARP SHOOTER!

Aiiieee!

Archerfish catch their prey by squirting water! They usually hit the target, which can be up to 5 feet (1.5 m) away, with their first shot. If the prey is close to the water, the fish can even leap out to grab it with its mouth.

Gotcha!

Snakes can survive for six months without eating.

A chameleon's tongue can be as long as its body.

oooof!

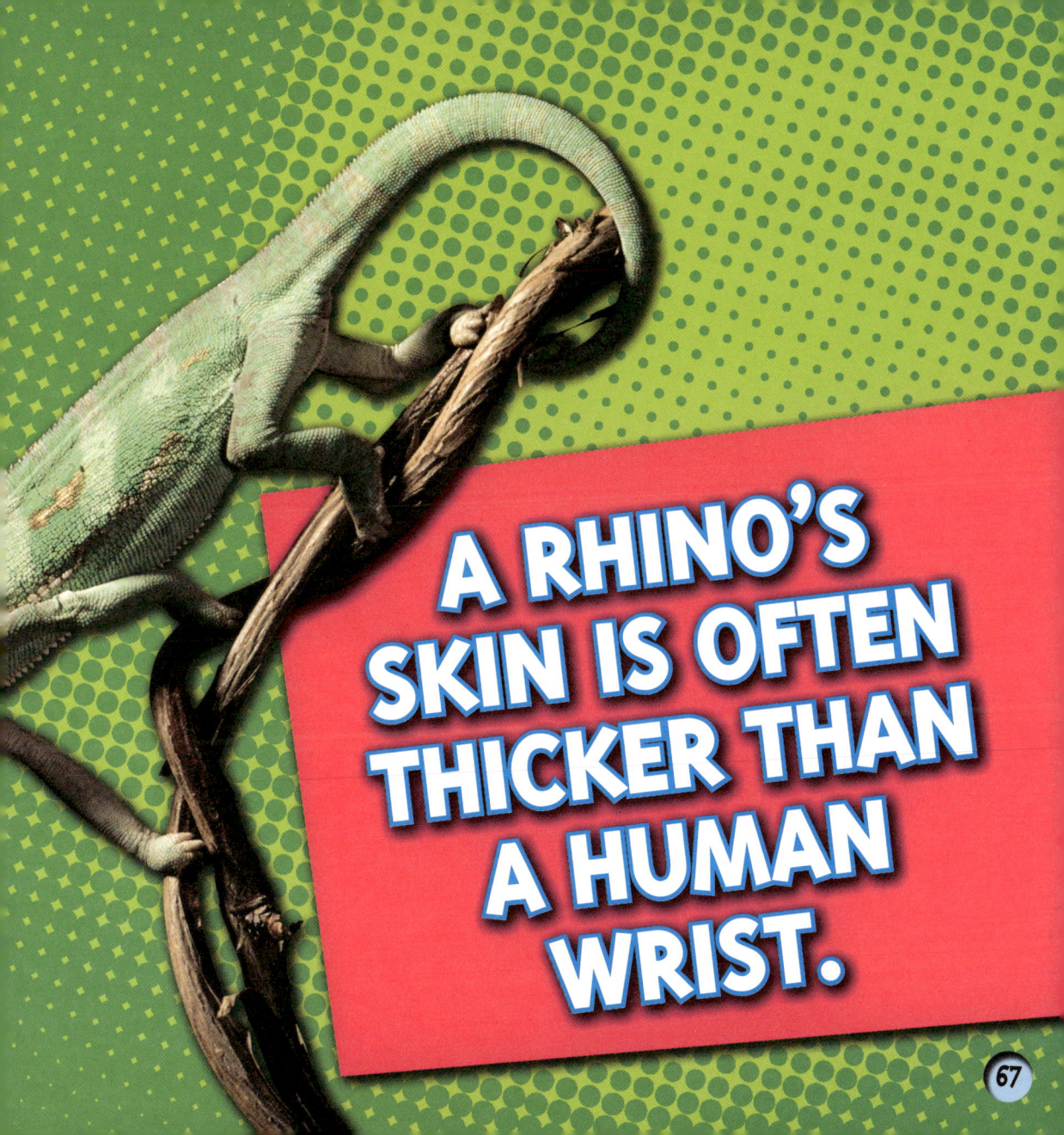

A RHINO'S SKIN IS OFTEN THICKER THAN A HUMAN WRIST.

Damselflies have two **HUGE** eyes that are made up of about 30,000 lenses.

The oldest **goldfish** on record was **over 40** years old.

An **elephant's trunk** has more than **40,000** muscles.

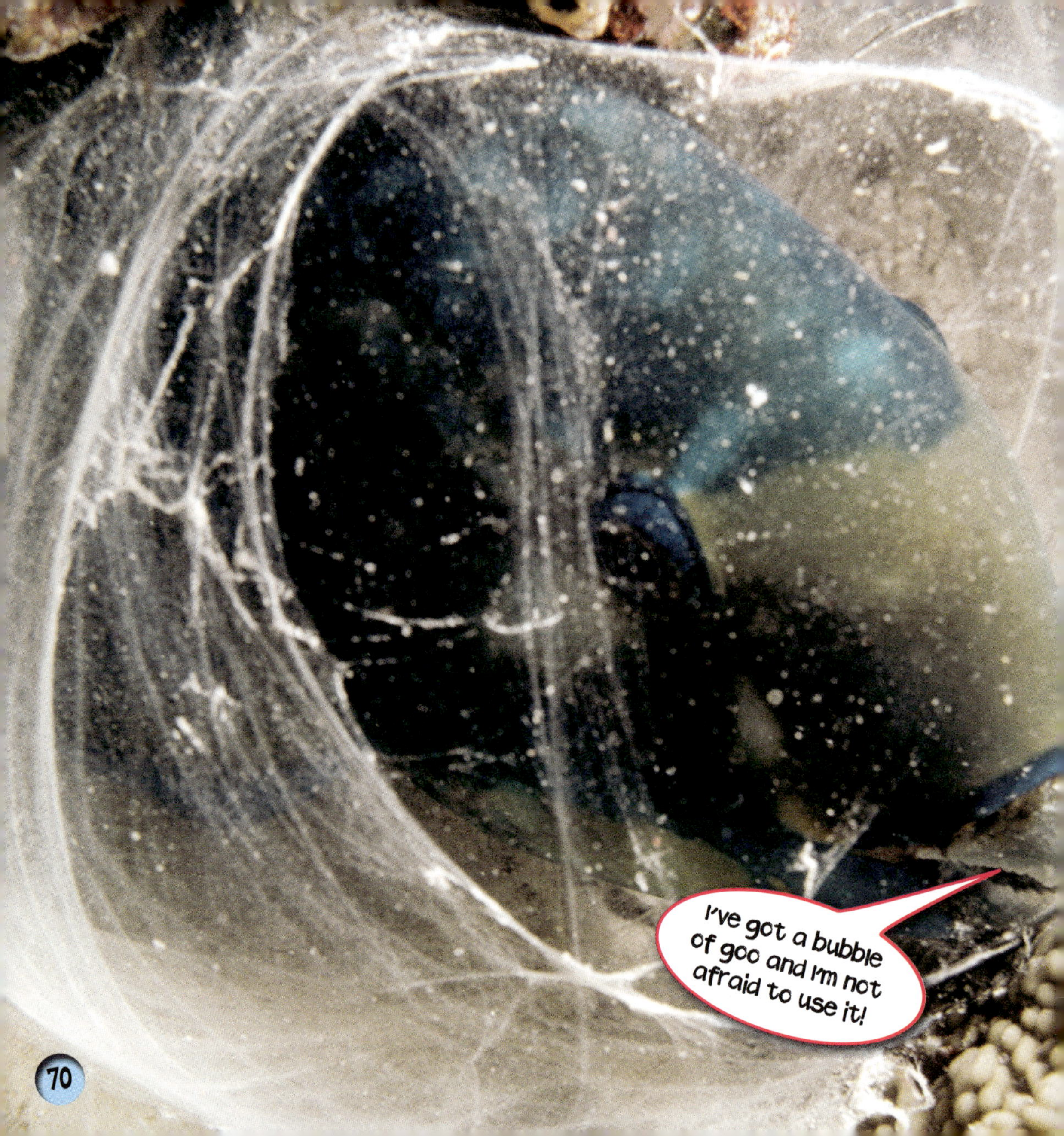
I've got a bubble of goo and I'm not afraid to use it!

SUPER-GOO

Parrotfish blow their own bubble of goo to protect themselves at night. It keeps away parasites that bite them and suck their blood.

★ A bee produces only half a teaspoon of honey during its lifetime.

A giant squid has teeth...

...in its tentacles!

The tentacles grab its prey and the teeth grip it so it can't escape.

Awesome!

MR. GREEDY!

Male gorillas can eat over 40 pounds (18 kg) of grass, leaves, and roots a day. That's the same as you eating **500** bags of potato chips.

Phaaarp!

GREAT WHITE SHARKS CAN ROLL THEIR EYES BACK IN THEIR HEAD FOR PROTECTION.

Giraffes and mice both have seven bones in their neck.

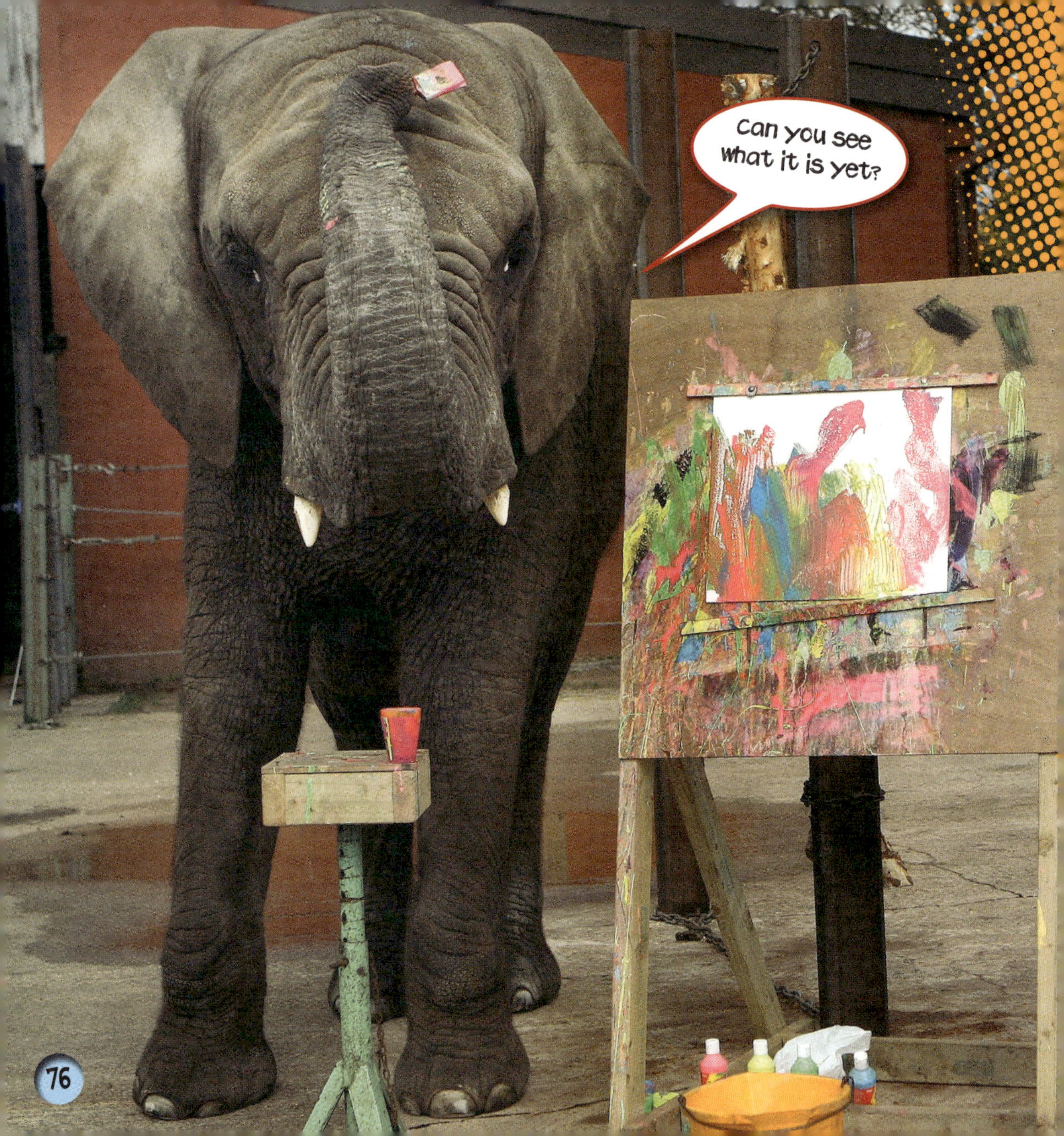
can you see what it is yet?

ELEPHART!

Five is an artistic elephant who lives at a safari park in the U.K. She has painted more than 50 beautiful pictures by holding the brush in her trunk.

HIPPOS ARE COVERED IN RED SLIME!

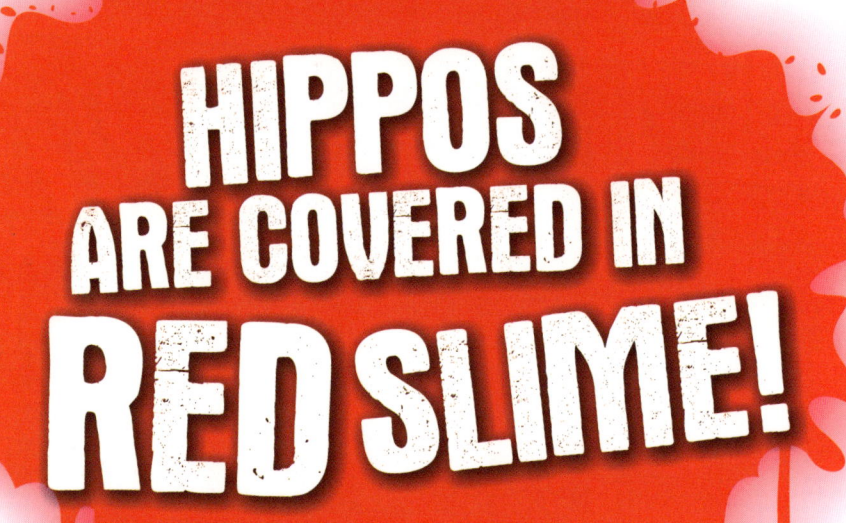

Their skin produces rosy-red goo, which acts as a sunblock.

Kangaroos are good swimmers!

Geckos lick their eyes to keep them clean!

This is because most of them don't have eyelids.

MEET THE FUNNIES
Introducing a few of nature's jokers...

Wow, check out that mohawk!

Eucharitid wasp

Elvis bug

Monkey grasshopper

Has somone been messing about with the highlighter pen?

WONDER WEBS!

...98, 99, 100. coming, ready or not!

82

Spiders spun some amazing webs when escaping from floods in Australia. As the waters rose, the spiders scuttled out of the way, climbing up trees and bushes spinning their webs as they went.

NON-SLIP SLIPPERS

I can't believe we both bought the same slippers!

Polar bears' feet have thick tufts of fur, strong claws, and little bumps to stop them from sliding on the ice!

GOTCHA!

Net-casting spiders spin a web of thick silk, which they use as a net to throw over their prey.

A new born joey (baby kangaroo) is so small it could fit into this teaspoon.

A **squirrel** in the U.K. squeezed inside a bird feeder and ate so many peanuts it **couldn't get back out** between the bars!

Anteaters are able to stick out their tongues up to **160** times a minute.

SPLIT ENDS

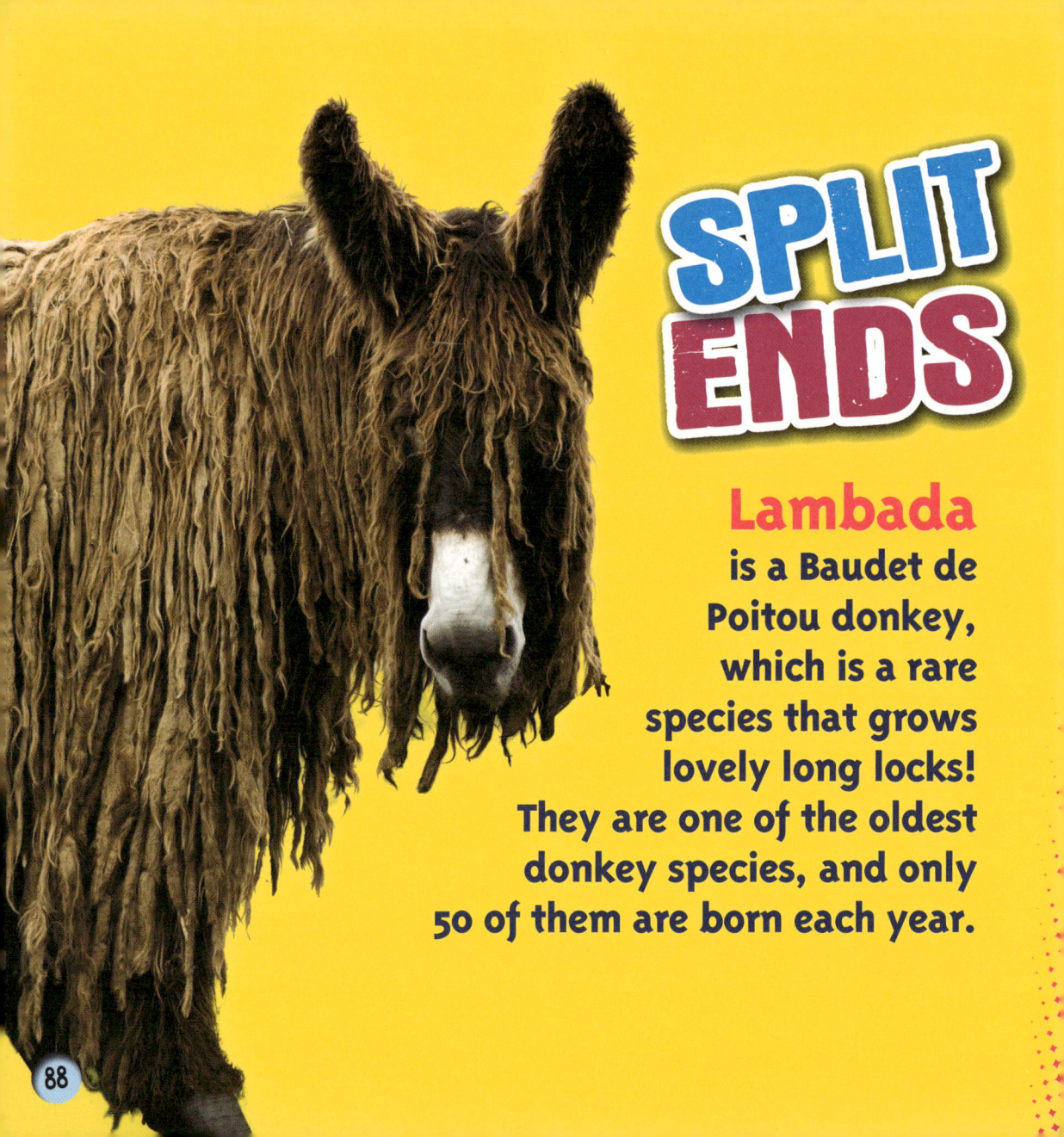

Lambada is a Baudet de Poitou donkey, which is a rare species that grows lovely long locks! They are one of the oldest donkey species, and only 50 of them are born each year.

SOME CATS HAVE FOUR EARS!

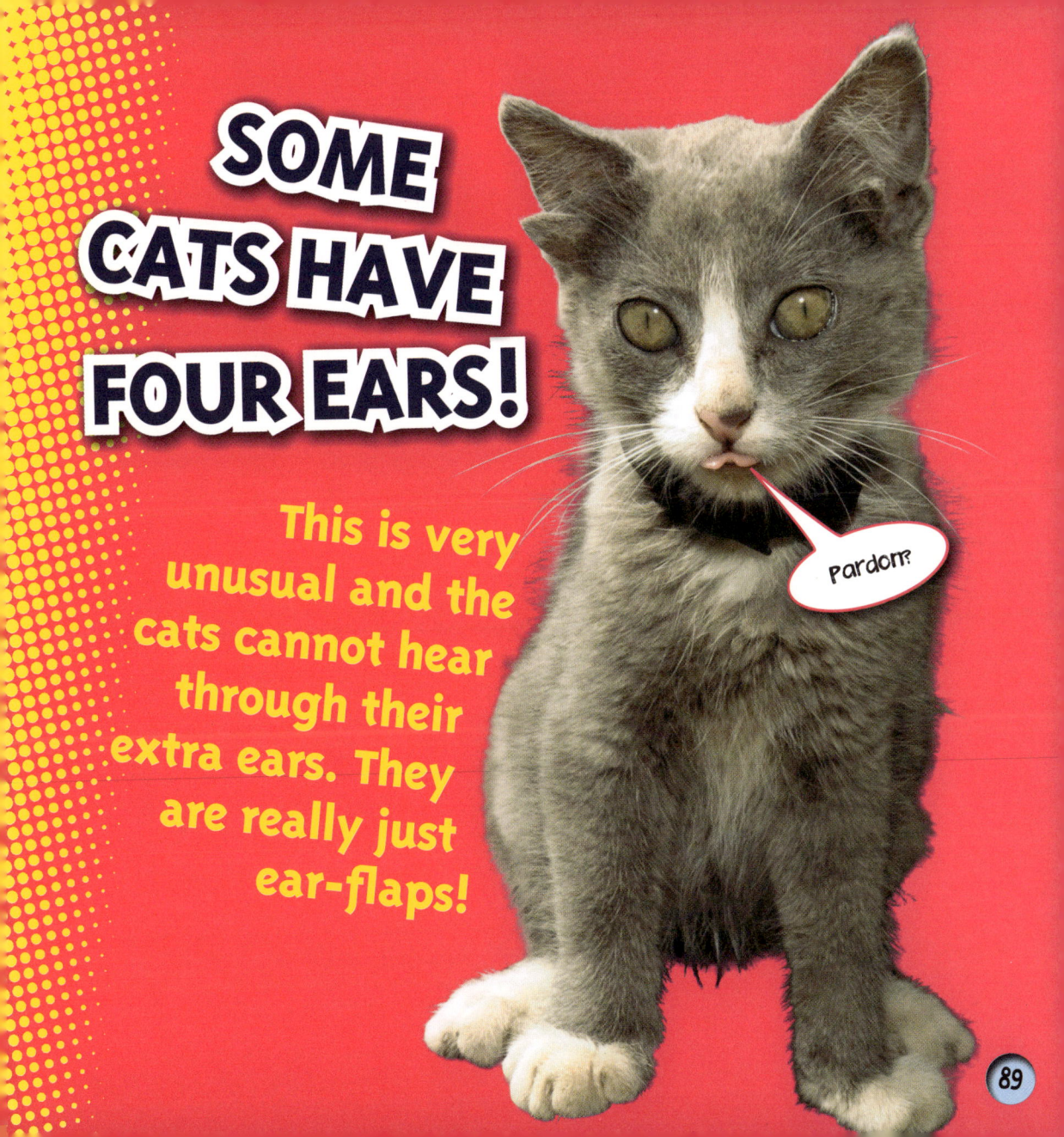

This is very unusual and the cats cannot hear through their extra ears. They are really just ear-flaps!

Pardon?

SCARFACE

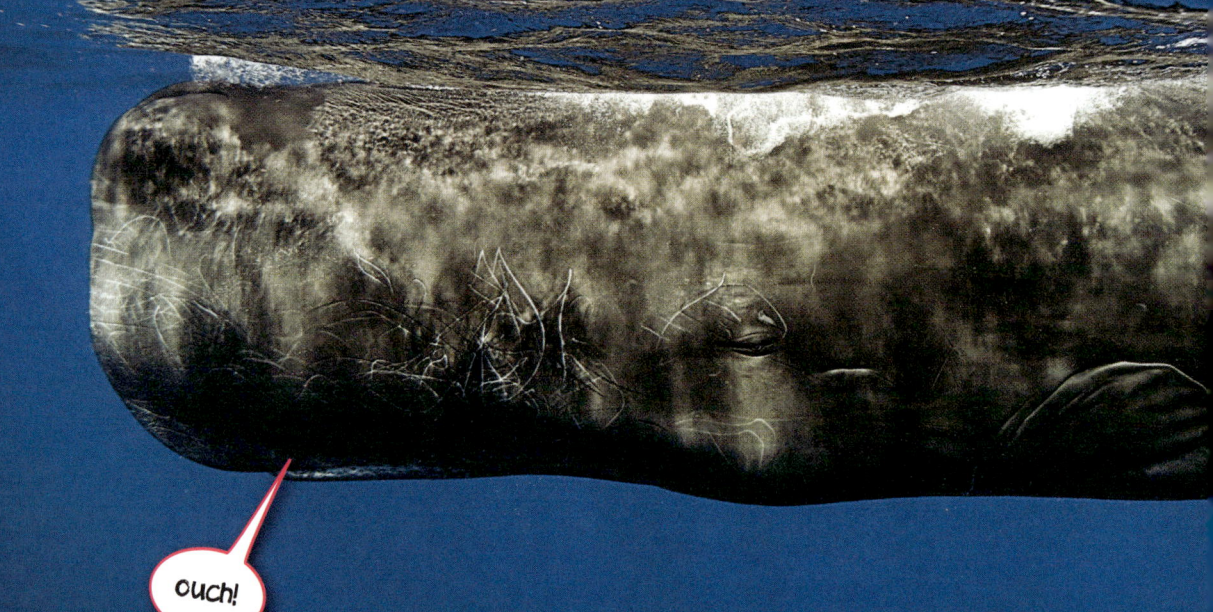

ouch!

Sperm whales are often scratched and scarred by fights with their largest prey, the giant squid and the colossal squid.

HALF-PIPE HOUND!

Tillman the bulldog loves to ride his skateboard around his home city of Los Angeles. He plays on the ramps in skate parks and can also ride down stairs. Tillman even has his own line of hats and t-shirts.

Gonna get me some BIG air this time!

Barracudas keep fish prisoner if they aren't hungry enough to eat them straightaway.

Sea urchins can walk on their TEETH!

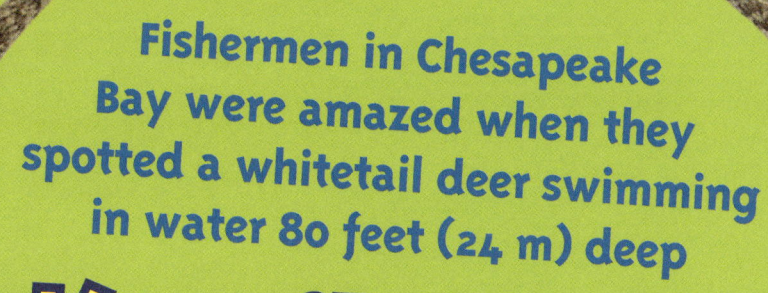

Fishermen in Chesapeake Bay were amazed when they spotted a whitetail deer swimming in water 80 feet (24 m) deep **1½ miles (2.4 km)** from shore. They lassoed it, lifted it into the boat, and took it back to dry land.

Step 1
Take a silly fluffy dog.

Step 2
Let it jump around in the snow.

Result:
Instant snowballs!

96

BRRRRRR!
(how not to make snowballs)

Kenzie the terrier couldn't wait to play out in the snow, **but look what happens when furry feet get frozen!** It's OK, one warm bath later and Kenzie's paws were defrosted and **back to normal.**

SOME CATERPILLARS HAVE 12 EYES.

Each head of a rare **two-headed** snake can fight over food.

GONE WITH THE WIND

When a storm struck Michigan, a 5-pound (2.3-kg) Chihuahua called Tinkerbell was picked up by a gust of wind and blown away. She was discovered unharmed two days later half a mile away in a forest.

wheeeee...

wow, look at those chops FLAP!

PARA PUG

Otis is a pug in a parachute that just loves to freefall! He wears special "doggles" to protect his eyes, and makes each jump in a harness strapped to his owner. He has been jumping for nine years and loves it.

MEET THE UGLIES
Feast your eyes on the world's worst...

He's going to grow up to be a lovely parrot...really?

Nelson, a baby Kea parrot, will grow up to have olive-green and orange feathers.

Rascal, a Chinese crested pure breed, won California's ugly dog contest.

Nancy the cat has been nicknamed "the gremlin".

Ooooh, look at those evil eyes!

103

104

BIG mama

Wolf spiders carry their babies on their back!

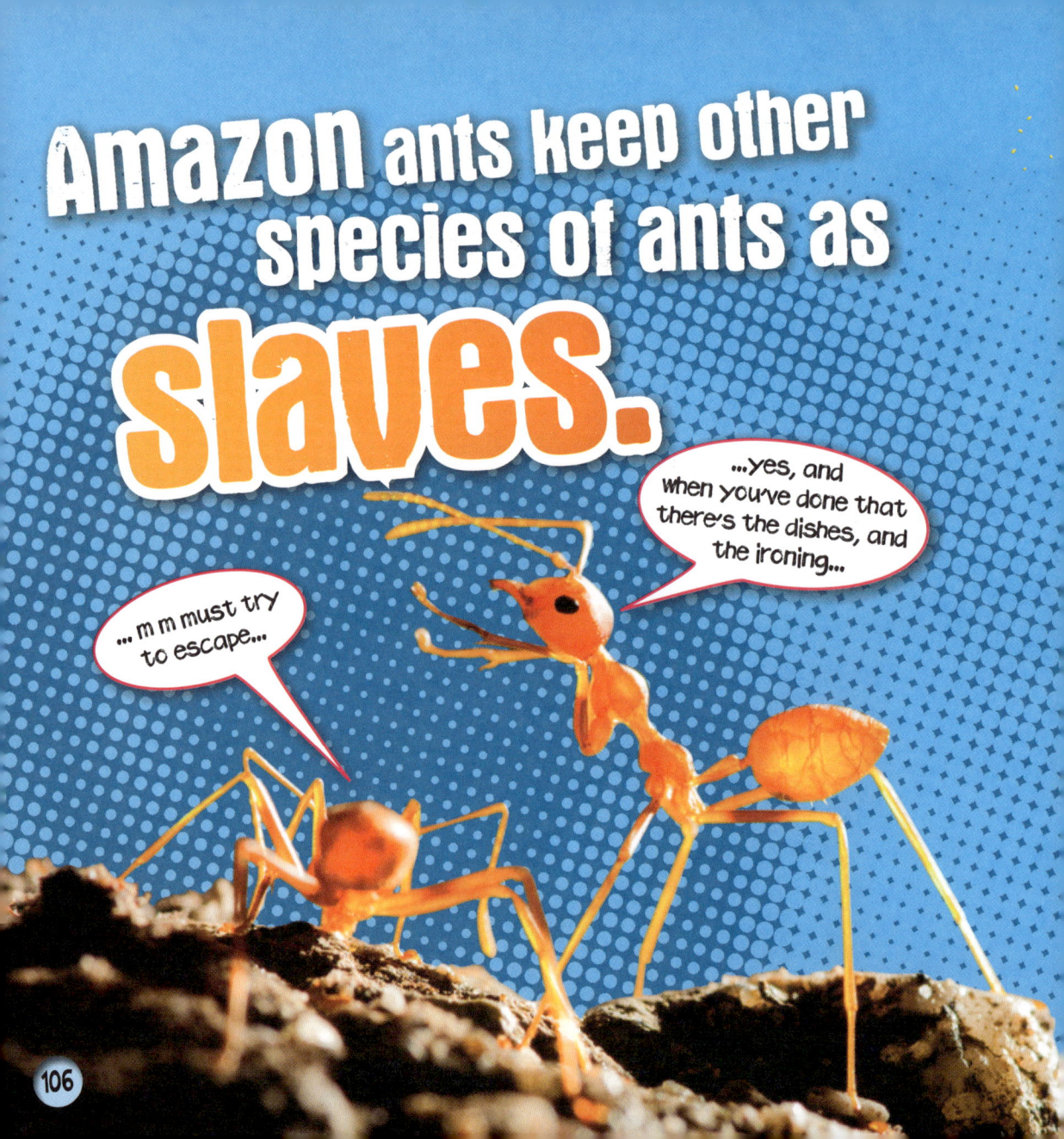

Amazon ants keep other species of ants as slaves.

...yes, and when you've done that there's the dishes, and the ironing...

...m m must try to escape...

Insects don't have blood. They are filled with a **GREEN** or yellow goo!

CATS ALWAYS WALK ON TIPTOE.

IF YOU GO DOWN TO THE WOODS **TODAY...**

Now where are we going?

Wildlife experts dress up in giant panda costumes to look after panda cubs.

WHY?

These cubs in China will be released into the wild when they are ready. They need to have as little human contact as possible, so their keepers put on the costumes whenever they need to handle the cubs.

BALD EAGLES CAN SWIM!

A shark cannot move if it is flipped upside down.

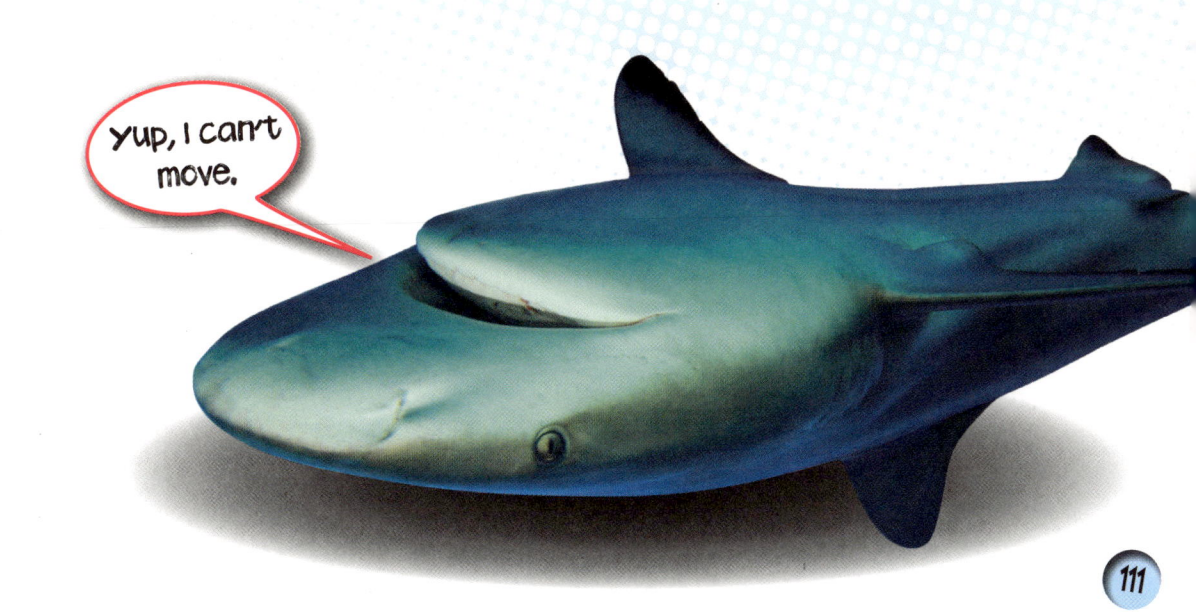

Yup, I can't move.

QUACKERS!

Could someone help take our hats off?

Visitors to the Sydney Family Show in Australia can watch ducks wearing dresses, hats, and ball gowns. The grand finale of the fashion show features a duck bride and groom in full wedding gear!

I've got cold feet!

Darling, come back!

Cows produce more milk when listening to music.

Ribbon worms can eat 95 percent of their own bodies if they cannot find food—and still survive!

DOG-GONE!

A four-year-old boy from England decided his week-old cocker spaniel needed a bath, so he put the dog in the toilet **and flushed it!** Plumbers found and rescued the tiny puppy in a waste pipe 20 yards (20 m) from the house.

Poor pup!

To boldly go where no chicken has gone before!

A rubber chicken called Camilla was sent into space in a spaceship made from a lunchbox! She was attached to a helium balloon and launched by students from a school in California as part of an experiment to study weather in space. After 2½ hours, the balloon popped and Camilla parachuted safely back to Earth.

Camilla before her epic trip

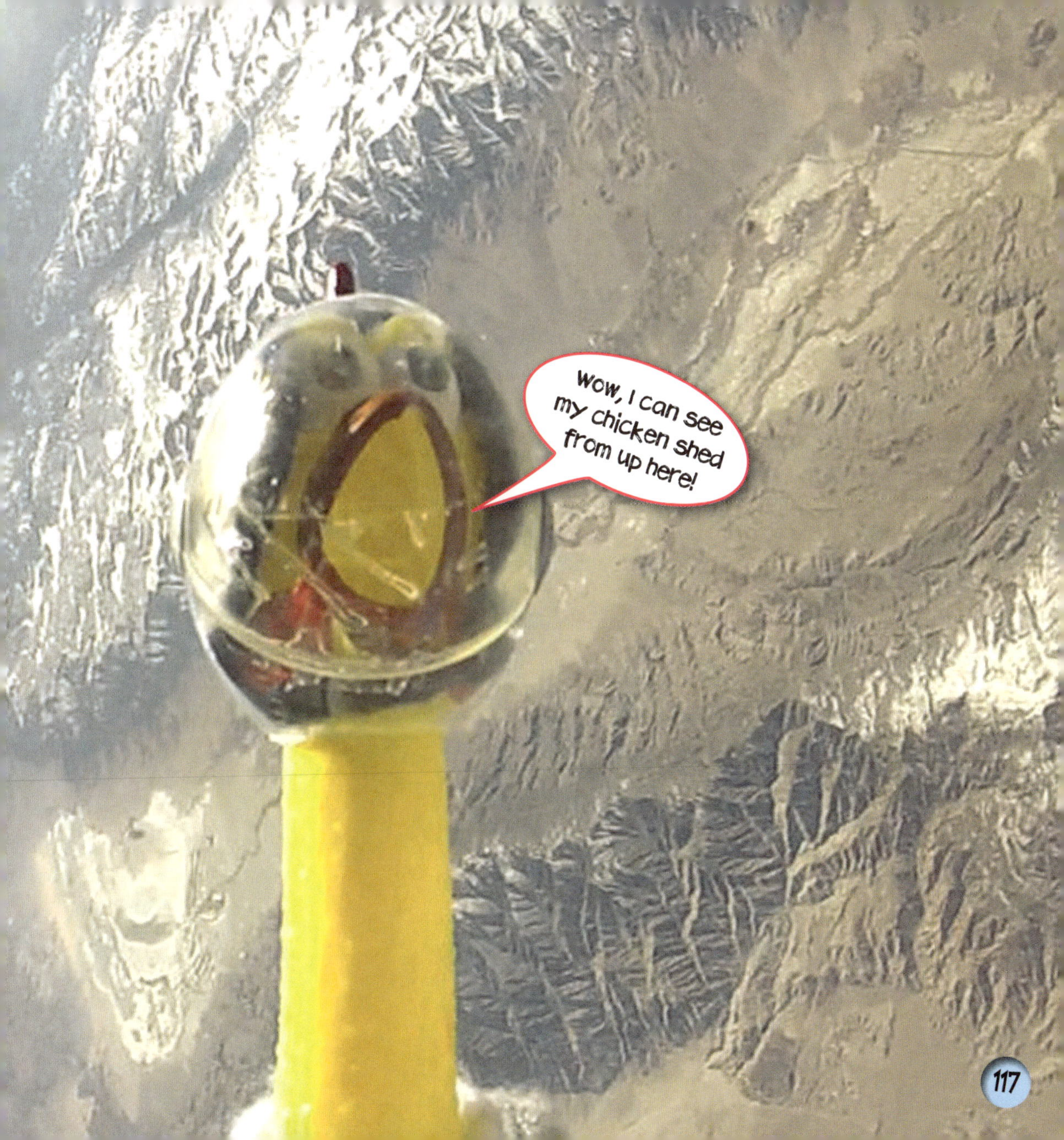
Wow, I can see my chicken shed from up here!

BAT WRAPS

ZZZZZZ

These baby bats were kept warm in little blankets after being rescued from the wild in Australia. A special bat nursery was set up to save baby bats who had been made orphans after serious floods in the area.

CLUMSY APES!

Approximately 50 percent of orangutans have **BROKEN BONES.** This is because they often fall out of trees.

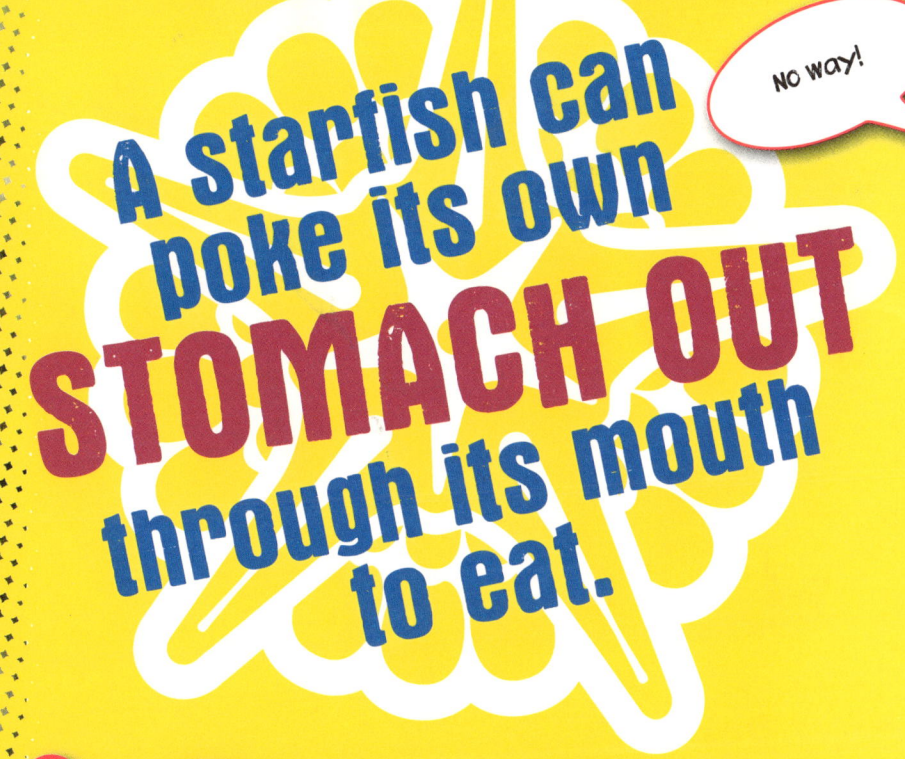

A starfish can poke its own **STOMACH OUT** through its mouth to eat.

No way!

Snails can sleep for three to four years at a time.

122

A group of penguins on land is called a **waddle.**

Some seals sleep for only 90 seconds at a time.

Polar bears can **smell humans** from 20 miles (32 km) away.

Moles can dig 75 feet (22 m) of tunnels in a day.

PURRFECT LUXURY

Craig Grant built a 30-acre (12 ha) cat sanctuary in Florida. It has cat-sized buildings including a city hall and police station! Caboodle Ranch is now home to 660 happy cats.

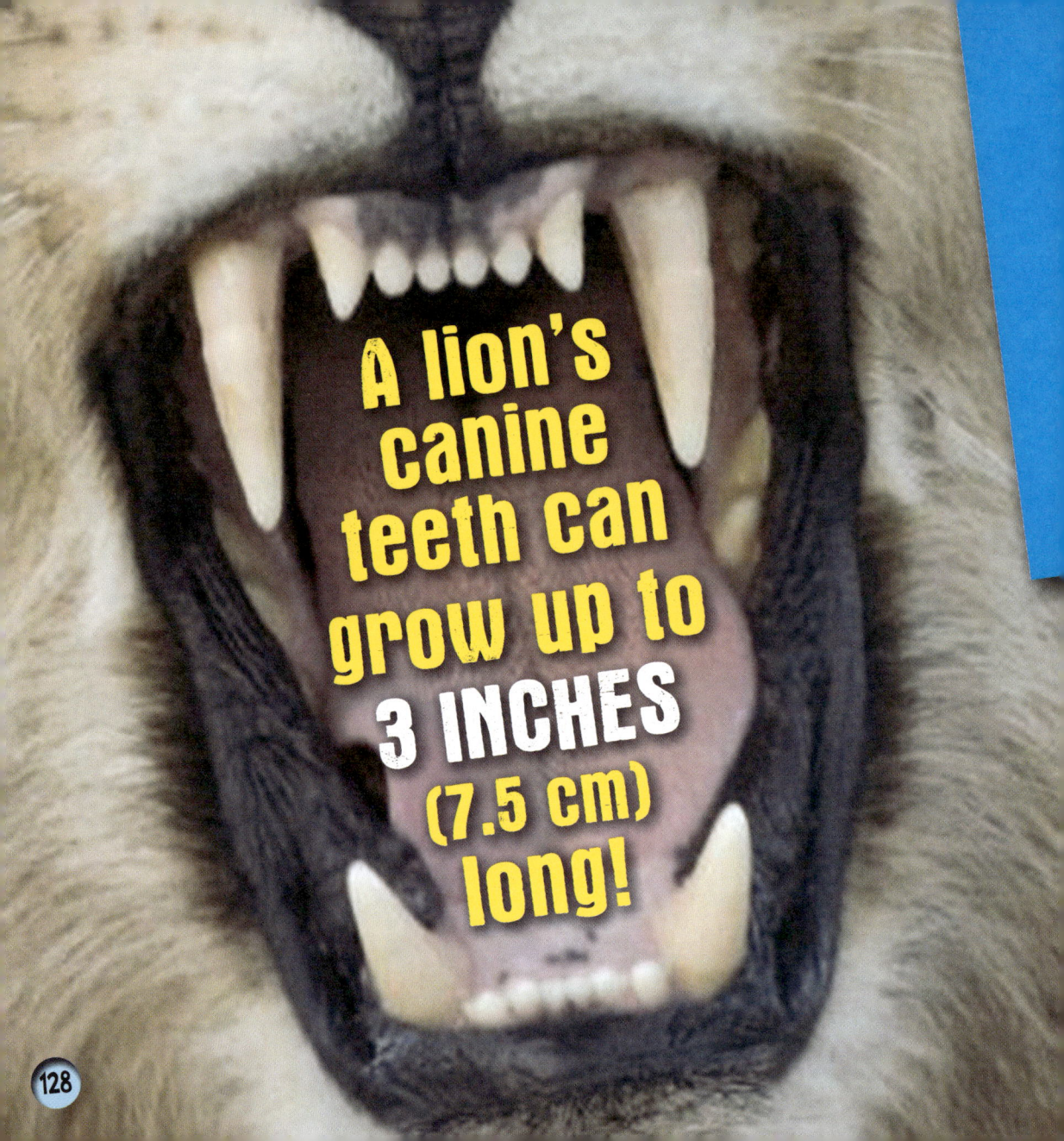

A lion's canine teeth can grow up to **3 INCHES** (7.5 cm) long!

A python can swallow a **whole** kangaroo.

Woooaah, indigestion!

When a Jack Russell terrier chewed up the mail at his home in England, the chewed glue and paper stuck his jaws together!

SWOOOSH!

c-c-can't stop!

Rollie the penguin liked skating so much he joined the National Rollerskating Association!

SQUELCH!

Race you to the top!

Schoolgirl Tiana Walton from England let 25 snails slither across her face. The nine-year-old said she found it relaxing, but the snails were a bit cold and smelly—and she could see their long eyes looking at her.

Wait for me!

FANCY A CUPPA?

What a hoot!

Two baby owls have found new homes in kitchen cups! The six-week-old owlets, named Linford and Christie, have moved in with wildlife park keeper Jimmy Robinson who is hand-rearing them at his home in England. They also like hiding in the dog basket and the bookcase!

Nice cup!

BEES CANNOT FLY WHEN IT RAINS.

A garden snail would take 95 YEARS to slide around the world. Garden snails move at a pace of ½ inch per second (13 mm/sec) and are the fastest snail movers.

DEER ME!

Connie Beck woke one morning to hear strange noises in her home in Pennsylvania. When she went to look, she found a deer taking a bubble bath in the bathtub! Not only had the deer broken into the house, it had also managed to turn on the water, knock over a bottle of bubble bath, and climb into the tub!

THEY'RE NUTS!

Now, which ones are mine?

Acorn woodpeckers spend hours pecking hundreds of holes in tree trunks. They then pick acorns from oak trees and carefully fit them into a hole that's just the right size.

Alligators can be *hypnotized* in 30 seconds by turning them over and putting pressure on their necks.

SHARKS HAVE NO BONES.

PHWOAR!

A spotted skunk often does handstands before it squirts its stinky spray. Its spray can reach up to **15 feet** (4.5 m) and is used to scare off enemies.

Take that!

TEAM BUILDING!

Ants link together to make a bridge so their friends can cross a gap!

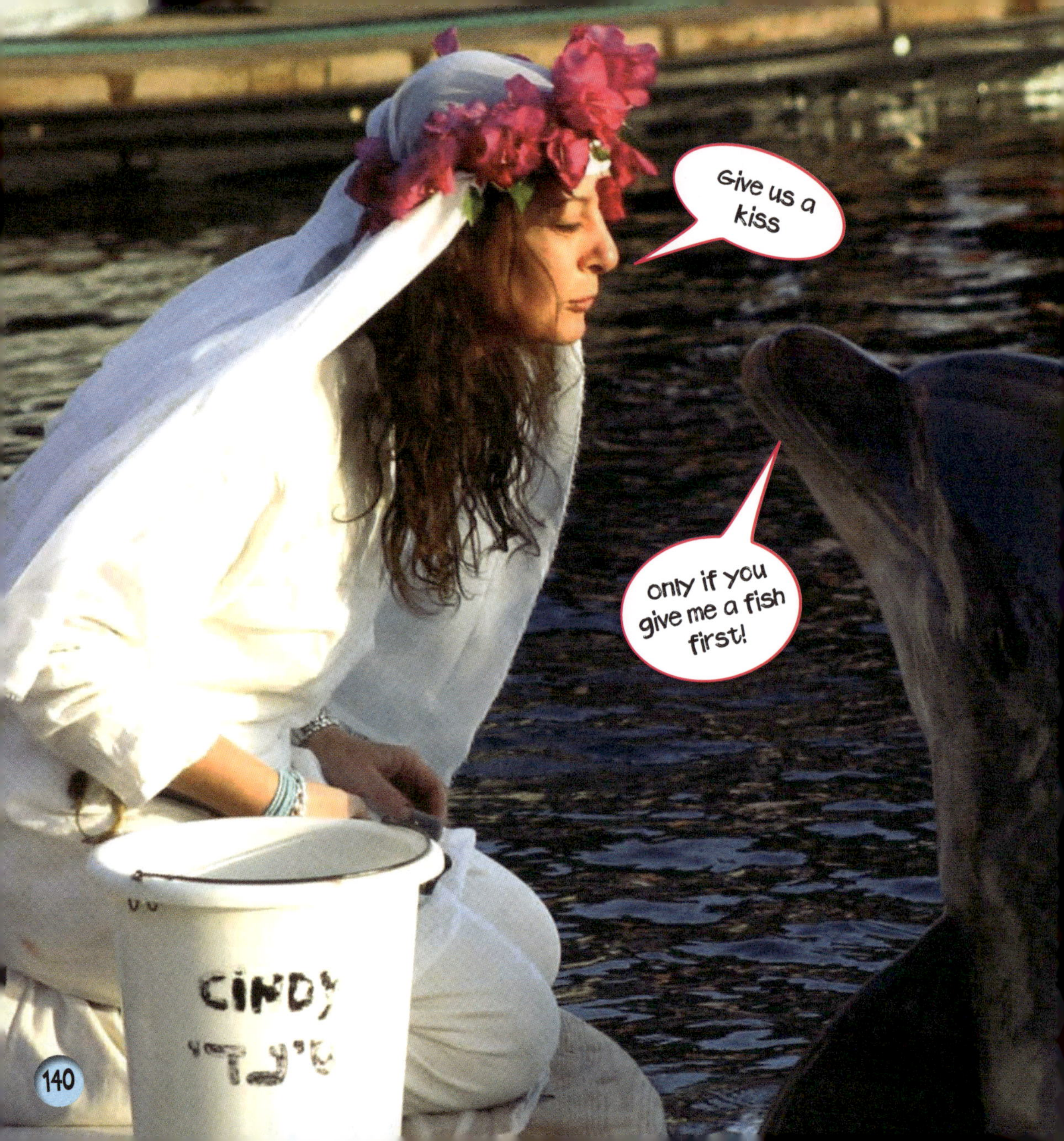
Give us a kiss
only if you give me a fish first!

DOLPHIN'S BRIDE!

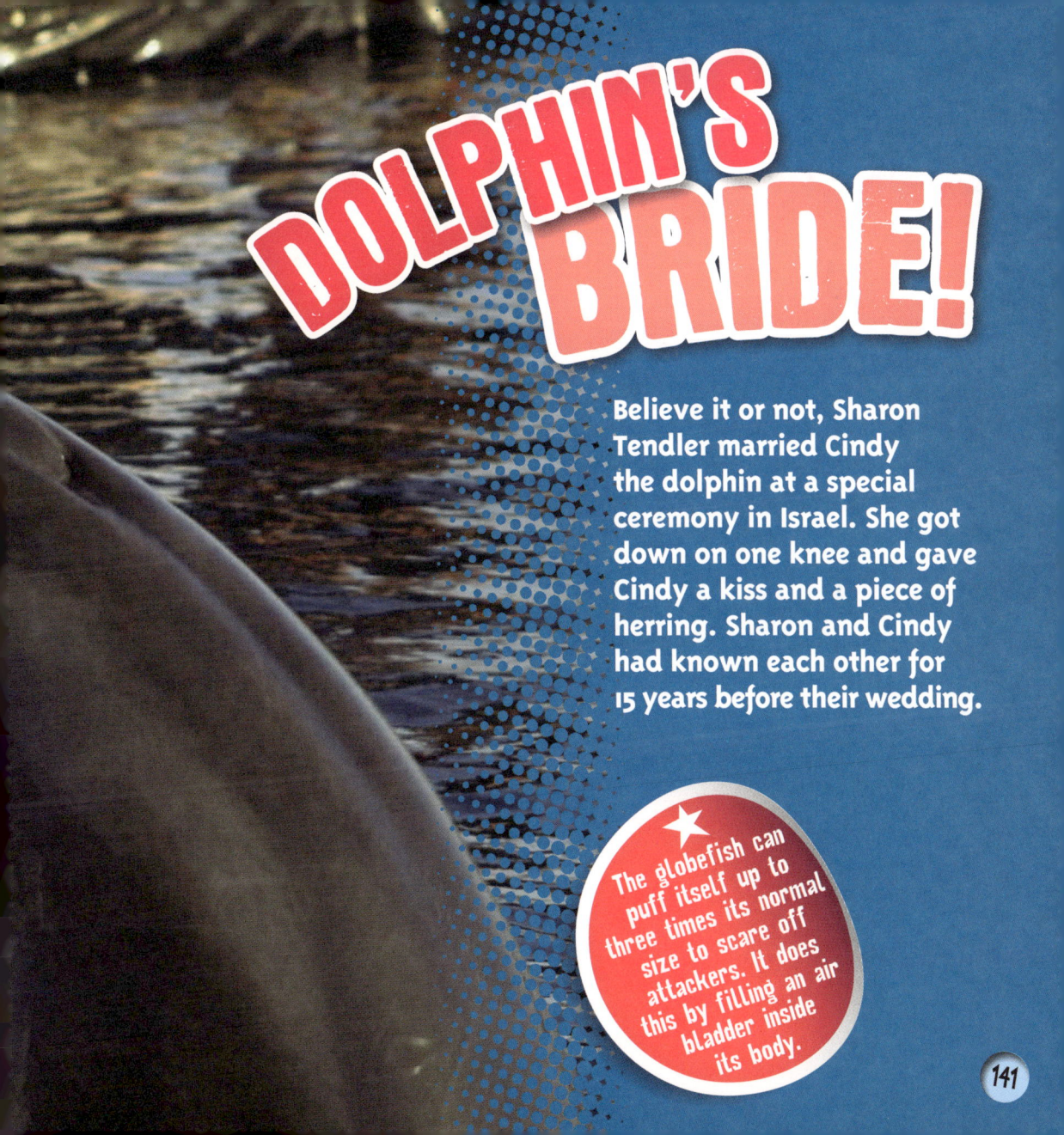

Believe it or not, Sharon Tendler married Cindy the dolphin at a special ceremony in Israel. She got down on one knee and gave Cindy a kiss and a piece of herring. Sharon and Cindy had known each other for 15 years before their wedding.

The globefish can puff itself up to three times its normal size to scare off attackers. It does this by filling an air bladder inside its body.

A starving mouse will eat its own tail.

Giraffes can lick their own ears!
Their tongue is more than 12 inches (30 cm) long.

Boxer crabs have claws that really STING!

HOW COME?

The crab grabs sea anemones and holds them in its front claws as extra weapons to fight off its enemies.

Comin' atcha!

Some fish swim together in huge shoals, or schools, containing thousands of fish.

Stop pushing!

Oi, move over!

Anyone seen Fred?

Fish use their eyes and a row of pores running along their sides to help them swim so closely together. Special hairs in their pores sense changes in the water from the movements of other fish or predators.

Koalas don't drink

No thanks mate, I don't drink.

WANT TO KNOW WHY?

Koalas hardly ever have to drink because the only food they eat is eucalyptus leaves, which are 50 percent water. They can even tell the age of the leaves by their smell. Eucalyptus is so low in energy that koalas spend 20 hours a day asleep.

SOME FROGS DON'T HAVE EARS

Nope, none on this one

Panamanian golden frogs don't have outside ears—their lungs pick up sound waves and direct them to their eardrums.

Ooof, I feel a bit sick

A flamingo can only eat when its head is **upside down**.

A WALRUS has three times the sucking power of a **vacuum** cleaner. This might explain why its stomach is full of **small pebbles!**

An earthworm has no eyes, ears, or nose.

MINI MACS

These little lambs needed protection from harsh winter weather, so the farmer dressed them in bright red plastic coats! They helped keep the lambs warm, and scared off predators such as foxes.

LIVING FEAST!

The markings on the side of this caterpillar may look like smiley faces, but the creature has nothing to smile about! Parasitic wasps have laid their eggs inside and on it so that, when hatched, their larvae have a ready-made lunch!

Can somebody scratch my back?

20 million bats live in a cave!

There are so many bats in Bracken Cave, Texas, that it takes more than **three hours** for them all to leave.

Must fly, don't want to get caught in the evening rush!

Prairie dogs kiss and cuddle when they meet each other.

... but what about me? Always left on my own with nobody to cuddle... sob!

TRUE LOVE?

When angler fish breed, the tiny male fish grabs onto the larger female with its mouth, and never lets go! His body gradually joins with hers and he is stuck there forever!

Ouch, stop biting my butt!

Male angler fish are teeny!

FLY SWAT

This impala needs a spring clean! It was caught on camera with a fully-woven spider web stretching between its horns.

There's no flies on me!

Night night, dear

PARTNERS
Sea otters hold paws while sleeping to stop them from drifting apart.

When moles eat earthworms, they first squeeze them like a tube of **toothpaste** to push out their **SOILY POO!**

Gross!

Using its antennae a bee can locate an **apple** tree three miles (5 km) away.

Lottie the tortoise disappeared from her home in England in 2008. She was found **two years later**, just 1½ miles (2.4 km) away.

Mosquitoes prefer biting people with smelly feet.

She's up!

Ah, so that's why I always get bitten!

162

SAY WHAT?

Do goats faint? Believe it or not, they do! The fainting goat is a breed that goes stiff and falls over whenever it's startled. It remains still on the ground for about 15 seconds before it jumps up again.

She's up again!

She's down!

Greedy GUTS!

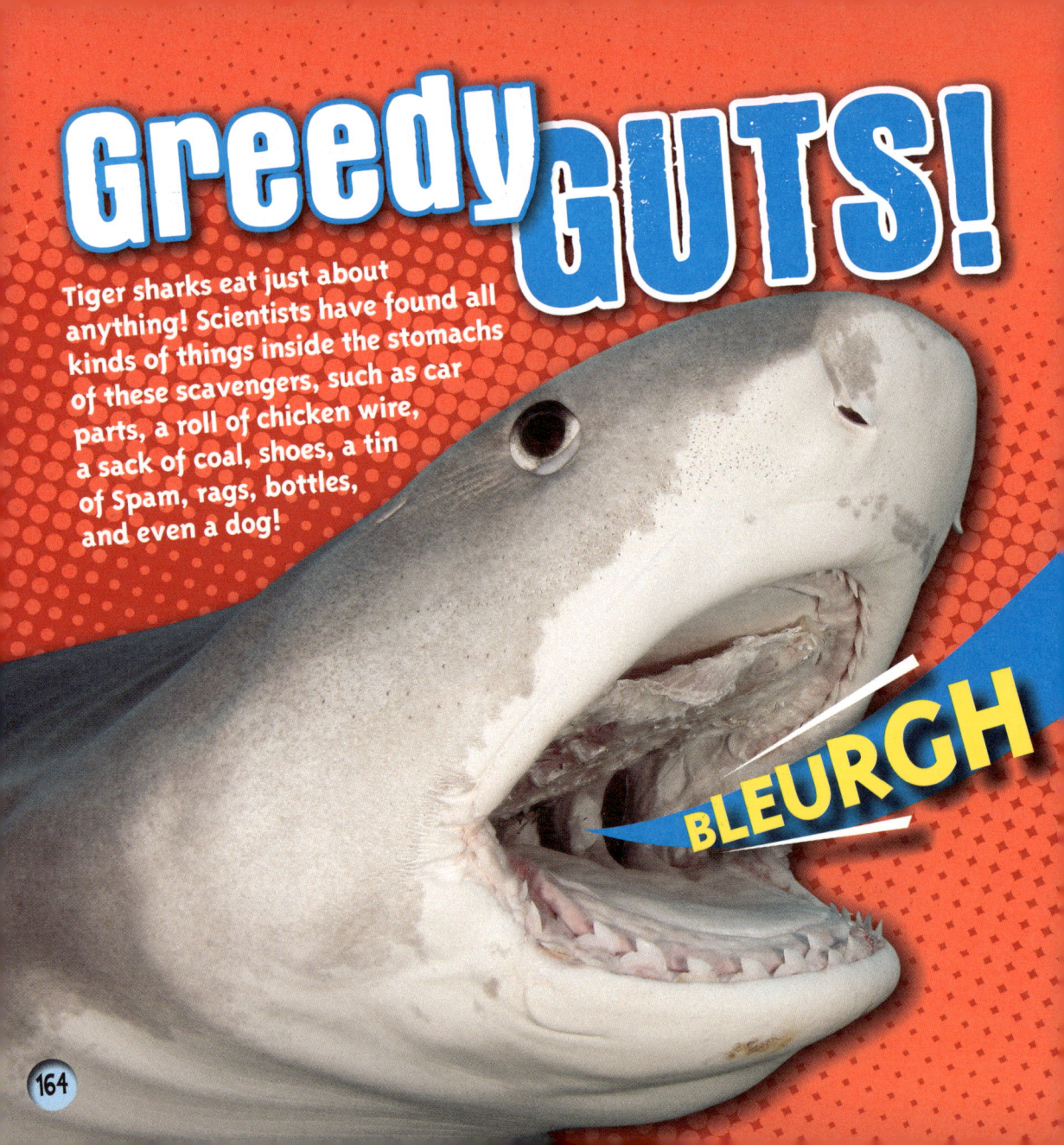

Tiger sharks eat just about anything! Scientists have found all kinds of things inside the stomachs of these scavengers, such as car parts, a roll of chicken wire, a sack of coal, shoes, a tin of Spam, rags, bottles, and even a dog!

BLEURGH

They look a bit cheesy!

A dog? Are you kidding?

I bet they were a bit rubbery!

OK, but not the tin as well!

DANGER COWS' TONGUES!

Cows caused a lot of damage to a house in Tennessee, just by licking it! They stuck their heads through their fence, which was just a few feet from the home of Jerry Lynn Davis, and broke a gutter and a screen window with their strong tongues.

GIZZA KISS!

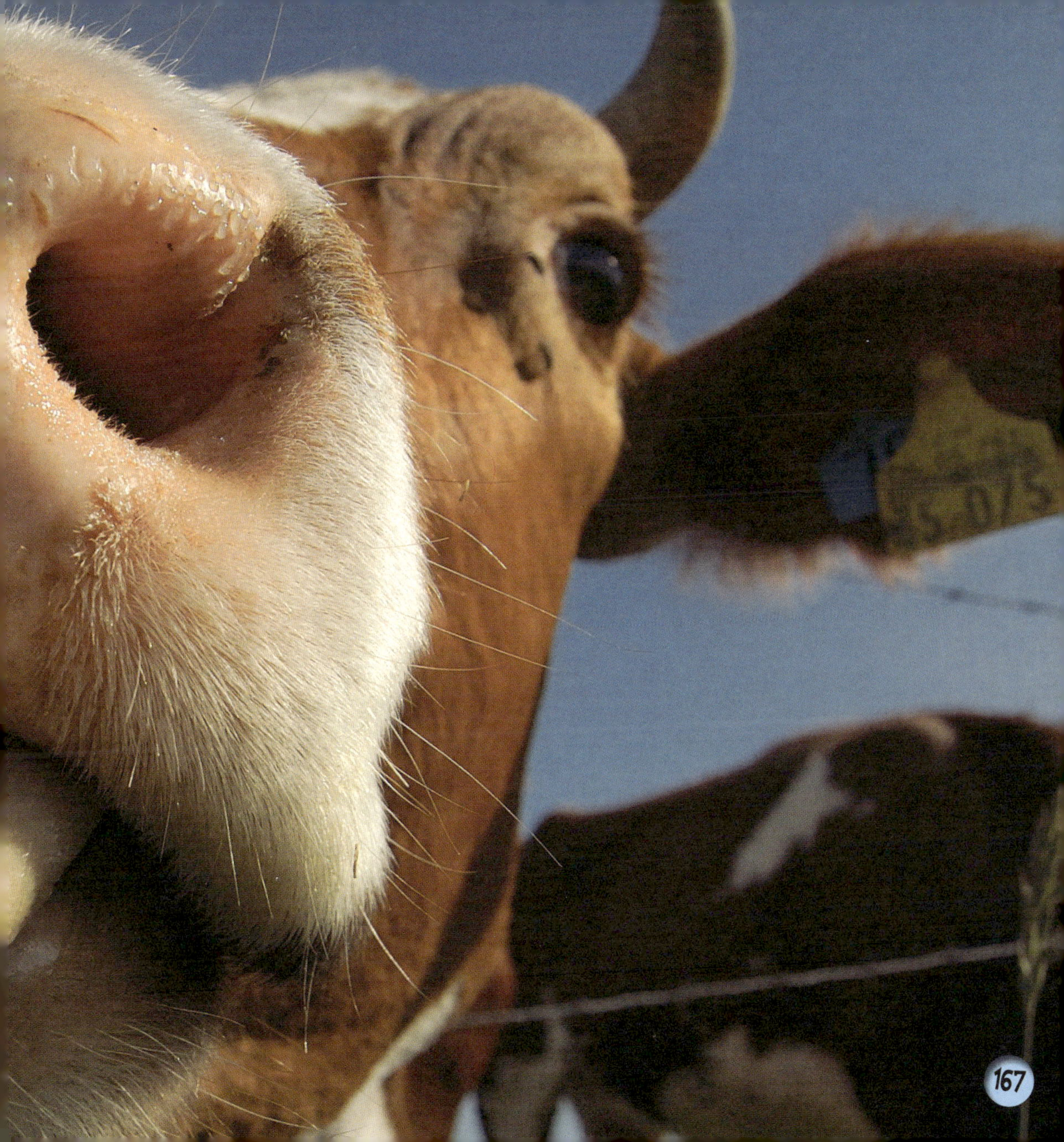

A hamster is able to carry half its own bodyweight in food in its cheeks.

cheeky!

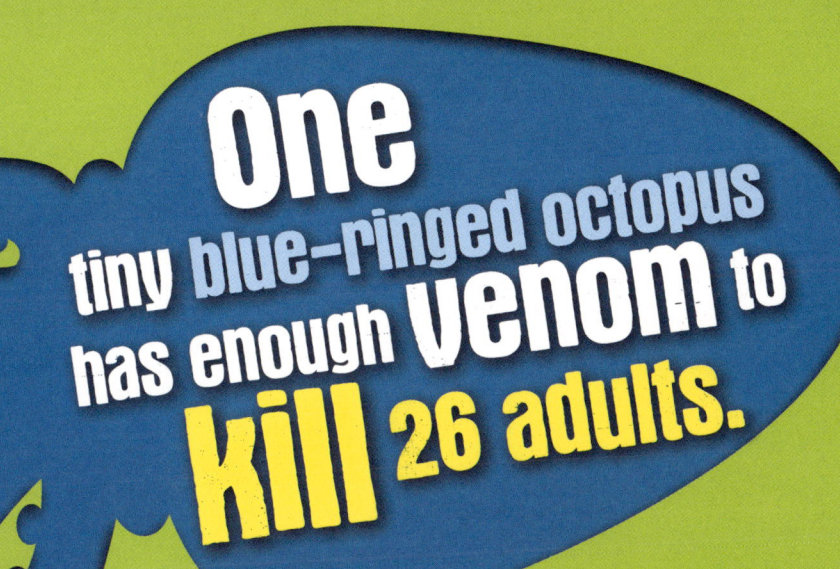

One tiny blue-ringed octopus has enough **venom** to **kill** 26 adults.

The nest of a bald eagle can weigh as much as **TWO CARS!**

A white cat with blue eyes is much more likely to be deaf than other cats.

New balls PLEASE!

ANYONE FOR TENNIS?

Auggie the dog liked to do tricks with tennis balls. Believe it or not, he could pick up **FIVE** tennis balls in his mouth at the same time!

Left, right, left... MARCH!

BLUNDER

TRIP

Hey, watch it!

172

Spiny lobsters use their long antennae to keep hold of the lobster in front as they march across the seabed. Sometimes more than 50 lobsters join the line to migrate each winter to warmer, calmer waters to lay their eggs.

Oooof!

Come on, come on, keep it up!

MEET THE GLOWIES

Deep, deep down on the dark ocean floor...

Cockatoo squid

...some animals create their own light. They use chemicals in their body or cover themselves in light-producing bacteria.

Ahhh, pretty!

Comb jelly

Red shrimp

Young gannets are fed so much fish that they are **unable to fly** when leaving the nest.

They **have to starve** for a couple of weeks until they are light enough to take-off.

An octopus has no skeleton and can "ooze" through an opening just bigger than its eyeball.

on your marks, set... GO!

An adult bear can run as fast as a horse!

Ahhh, I see the problem, a bent straw. He's not going to get very far unless...

SHHLURP!

...that's the way, careful now!

When Charlie the chipmunk was thirsty, he decided that a long, cool glass of freshly squeezed orange juice would do very nicely. So, Charlie sucked on the straw before diving head first into the glass and drinking it all!

SHOW OFF!

Jaguars have rough tongues that are designed to peel the skin away from the flesh of its prey.

Forget about the roughness, look at the size of the thing!

A crocodile cannot stick its tongue out.

A wolf's sense of smell is about 100 times better than a human's.

FINE DINING

Red-billed oxpeckers feed from the skin and ears of large African mammals, such as this impala. They like to eat blood-filled ticks, earwax, and snot. Yum!

YUK!

Why did the ducklings think their mother was a white ball?

Mama?

A scientist convinced a group of newborn ducklings that a white ball was their mama because ducklings think that the first moving object they see is their mother.

FANTASY FEST

Dogs were dressed up in some cool outfits for a pet masquerade contest in Florida. Some owners even wore matching costumes.

Really, who ever heard of a dog dressed as a lobster?

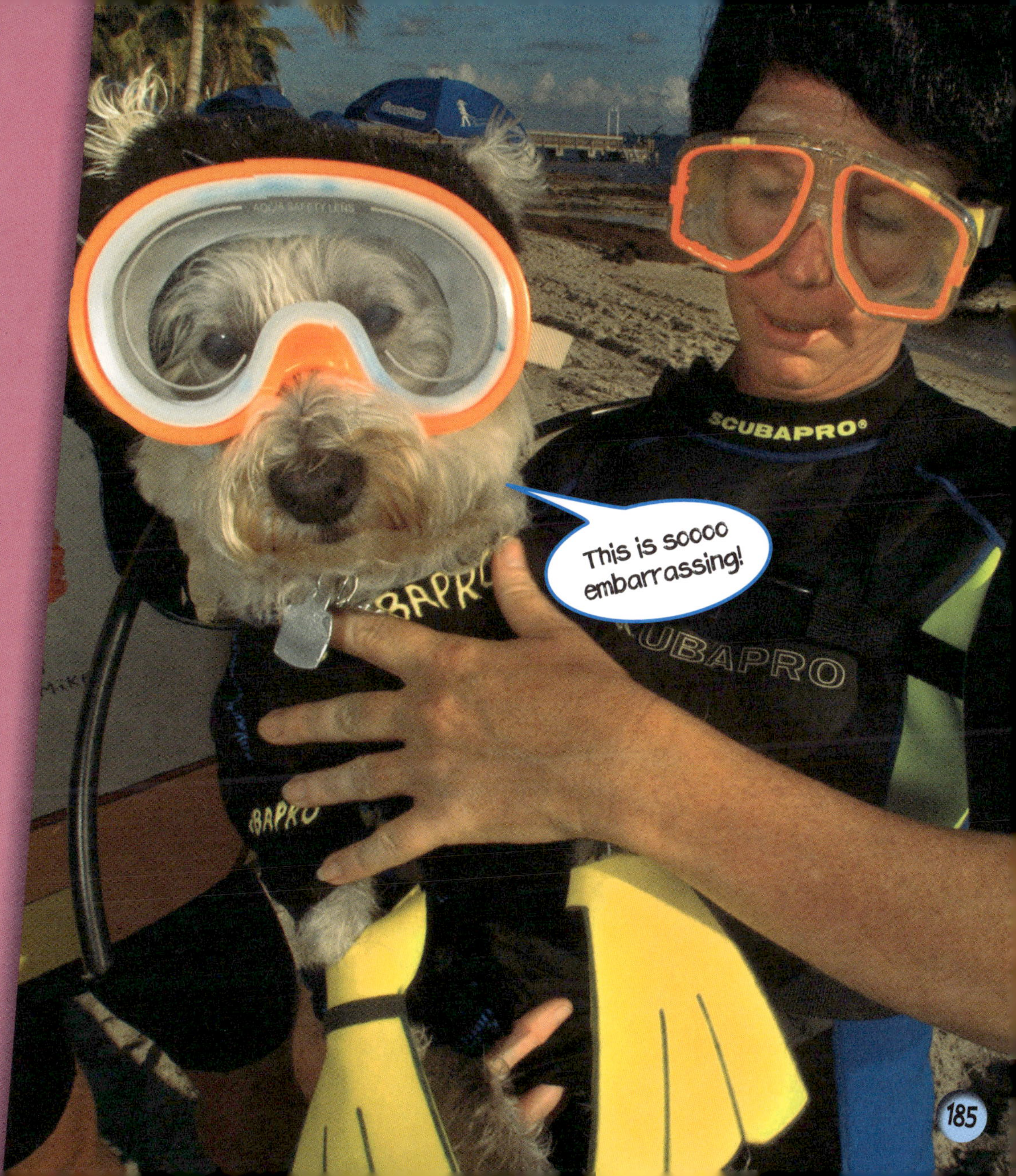
This is soooo embarrassing!

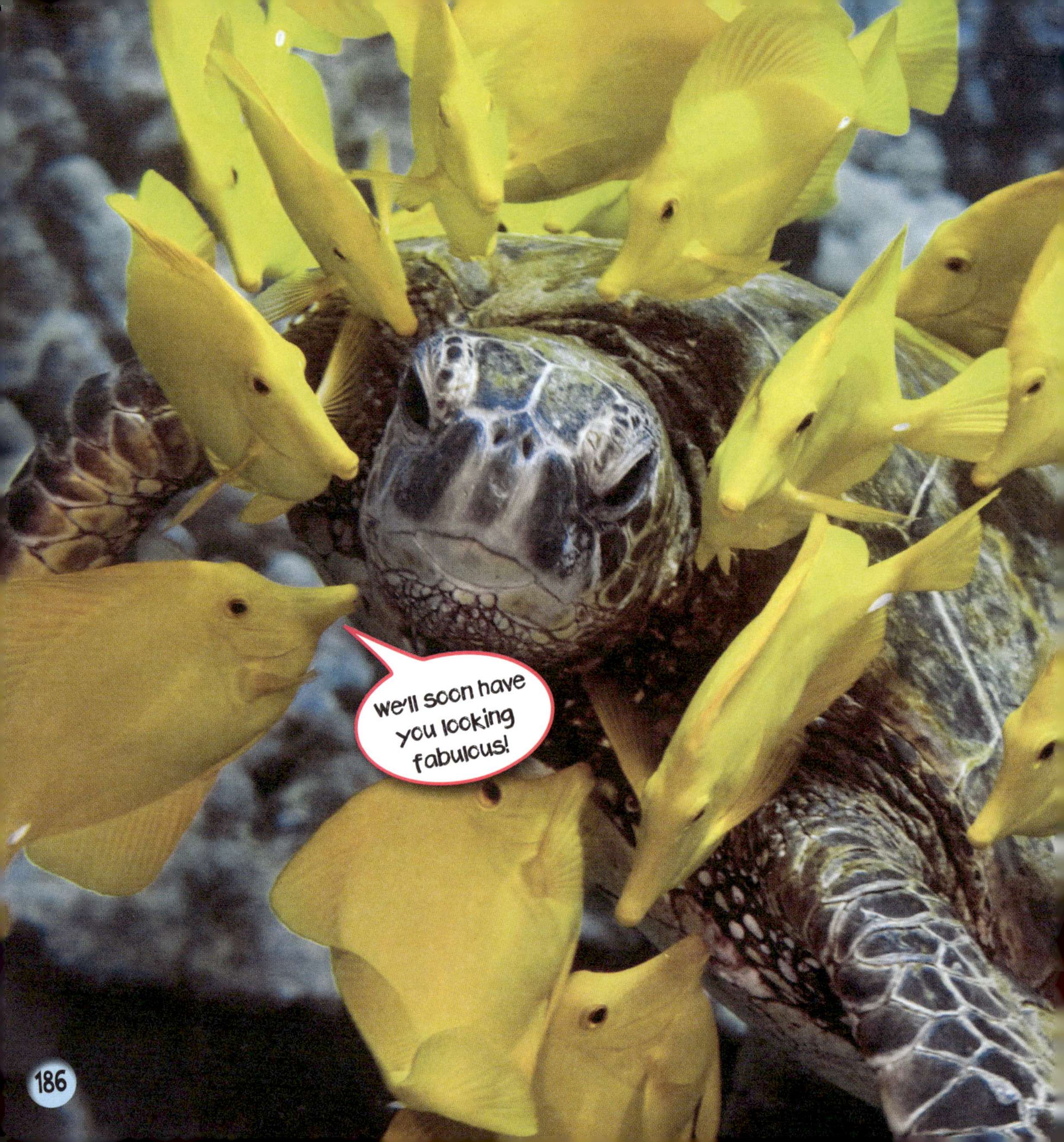
We'll soon have you looking fabulous!

DEEP CLEAN

Believe it or not, sea turtles visit underwater cleaning stations to have the algae removed from their shell and body. Schools of fish, such as these yellow tangs, clean up the turtles and send them on their way as good as new!

Hummingbirds are the only birds that can fly backward.

A mouse has 225 bones. A human has only 206.

Dolphins have more teeth than any other mammal. They can have up to 100!

Do I have to keep it stuck in for six minutes?

Armadillos can hold their breath for up to six minutes. This means they can stick their nose deep into the ground when hunting insects.

"Go, go go!"

Please make sure my kennel door is always locked – I can open them!

Step 1
Red unlocks the door.

THE GREAT ESCAPE

Step 2
Under cover of darkness, the boys make a run for it.

It's all clear, cover me!

A clever dog was able to free himself and his doggie friends from their kennels at a dogs' home. For several nights, Red the lurcher opened the kennel doors with his nose and teeth. The dogs would then head to the kitchen for snacks, which is where staff found them each morning. Cameras were set up to see how the dogs were escaping, and the game was up.

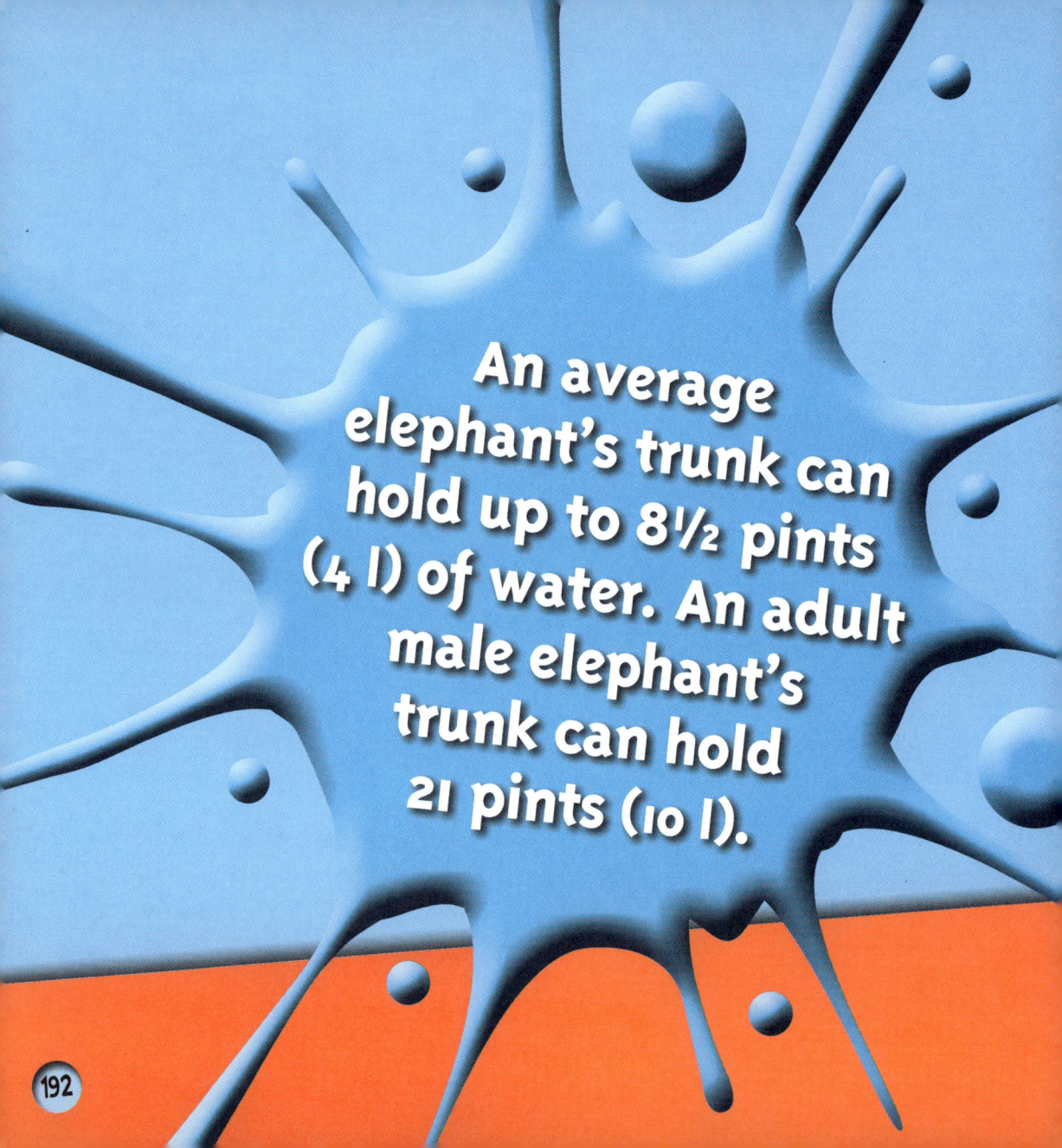

An average elephant's trunk can hold up to 8½ pints (4 l) of water. An adult male elephant's trunk can hold 21 pints (10 l).

There are more wild pigs than people in Australia. That's 21 million people and 23 million **pigs!**

Centipedes have an odd number of pairs of legs.

DANDY DOLPHIN

"I'm one of a kind!"

A bright pink albino bottlenose dolphin was spotted in a coastal lake in Louisiana. The dolphin, nicknamed "Pinky," is thought to be the only one of its kind in the world.

A catfish has more than a **quarter of a million** taste buds!

SAY WHAT?

The taste buds are not just in its mouth and gills, but on its whiskers, fins, back, belly, sides, and tail.

MR. BLOBBY

Hmm, I really must tone up.

The **BLOBFISH** lives in deep waters off the southeastern coast of Australia. Sadly, this weird-looking creature is facing extinction.

A CAT in Wales has 26 toes!

That's eight more than normal cats. The cat, named Des, has seven toes on each of his front paws and six on each of his back paws.

A hyena's mouth is so tough that it can chew a **GLASS BOTTLE** without cutting itself.

Leeches have **HUNDREDS** of tiny sharp teeth, and **5** pairs of eyes.

Yuk!

PORCUPINES CAN FLOAT IN WATER.

SLEEPING BEAUTY

Sperm whales sleep vertically.

201

A turtle with green hair?

This little guy was spotted swimming in an Australian river. It's an endangered Mary River Turtle and its crazy green "hair" is actually algae growing on its head.

Australian lyrebirds can imitate almost any sound, including chainsaws, phones, car alarms, barking dogs, and **crying babies.**

Anyone know where the nearest barber is?

203

SPOT THE FAKE!

I love you mama!

When four owl chicks were abandoned by their mother, keepers at a wildlife park in England gave them a stuffed toy owl instead. The babies happily snuggled under the toy's wings to keep warm.

YIPPEE!

No prizes for guessing why this little guy is called a **"happy face"** spider! These tiny, rare creatures measure around 1/5 inch long (5 mm) and are found in Hawaiian rainforests.

BIG MOUTH!

Male jawfish protect their eggs by keeping them inside their enormous mouths.

Sloths EAT, SLEEP, and GIVE BIRTH upside down.

"...which is cool, but when I eat I get crumbs in my eyes!"

One pat of elephant dung can contain up to **7,000** dung beetles.

Poo, bit whiffy!

WOW!

More than 307 million ants were once found in a single colony in Japan. There were 45,000 connecting nests built over an area of one square mile (2.5 sq km).

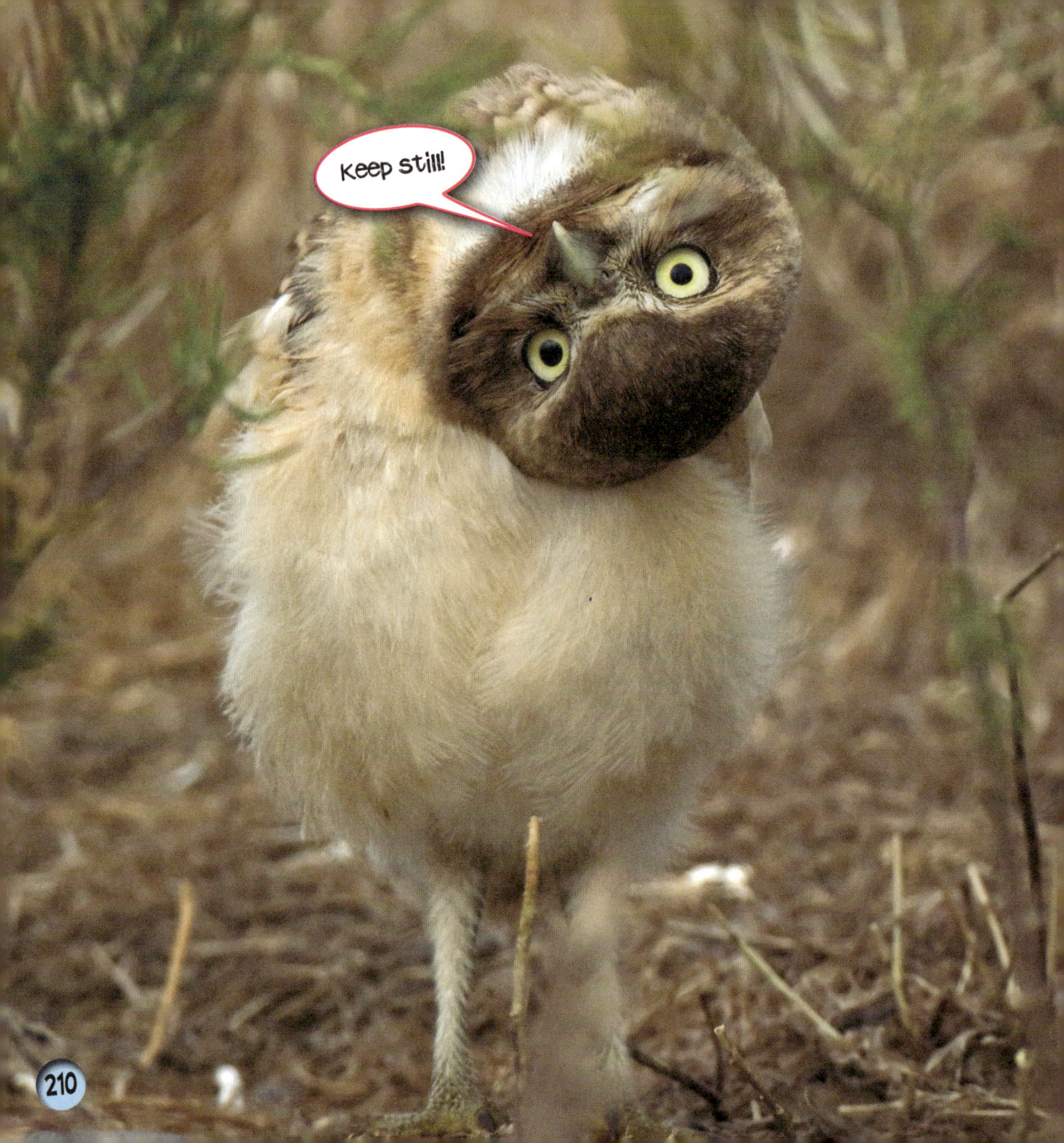
Keep still!

Whooo goes there?

Owls have **TEN TIMES** better hearing than you. They can also turn their head up to 270 degrees to help work out exactly where a sound is coming from.

MEET THE BALDIES

Take a deep breath and enter the bald zone...

Reggie, a baby baboon, went bald after his mother licked his head too often!

Spock the Dumbo rat was born bald.

Sphynx cats have no coat at all.

ARACHNID ARMY

Tens of thousands of harvestmen mass together and move as one giant scary creature!

A blue whale's aorta is so wide that an adult human could swim through it.

You would be in deep trouble though!

Aorta = the main artery that supplies blood to the body.

A male African elephant can weigh as much as 100 men!

Believe it or not, POLAR BEARS have black skin!

Honeybees have hairs on their eyes.

Where did I put my eye-brush?

INDEX

A
acorn woodpeckers 136
alligators 137
American bullfrogs 42-43
anglerfish 156-157
anteaters 87
ants 54-55, 106, 139, 209
archerfish 65
armadillos 189
Australian lyrebirds 202

B
baboons 212
bald eagles 110, 169
barracudas 94
bats 118-119, 154
Baudet de Poitou donkeys 88
bears 84, 125, 177, 217
bees 71, 134, 161, 218-219
birds 40-41, 45, 64, 102, 110, 122-123, 130, 132-133, 136, 148, 169, 176, 182, 187, 202, 204-205, 210-211
blobfish 196
blue whales 20, 216
boxer crabs 143
budgerigars 64

C
caterpillars 98, 152-153
catfish 195
cats 56-57, 89, 103, 107, 126-127, 170, 197, 213
centipedes 193
chameleons 66-67
chickens 46-47, 116-117
chipmunks 178-179
cockatoo squid 174
cockroaches 18
comb jellies 175
cows 12-13, 19, 45, 114, 166-167
crocodiles 7, 181
cuttlefish 61

D
damselflies 68
deer 95, 135
dogs 11, 15, 16-17, 45, 51, 92-93, 96-97, 99, 100-101, 103, 115, 129, 170-171, 184-185, 190-191
dolphins 140-141, 188, 194-195
ducks 38, 112-113, 183

E
earthworms 20, 149, 160
elephants 30, 69, 76-77, 192, 209, 216
Elvis bugs 81
eucharitid wasps 80

F
fish 4-5, 29, 45, 61, 65, 69, 70-71, 94, 141, 144-145, 156-157, 194-195, 196, 207
flamingos 148
flies 14
frogs 11, 42-43, 147

G
gannets 176
geckos 60, 79
giant squid 72-73
giraffes 75, 142
glass lizards 50
globefish 141
goats 26-27, 163
goldfish 69
gorillas 74
great white sharks 75

H
hamsters 168
happy face spiders 206
harvestmen 214-215
hippopotamuses 21, 28, 78
horses 9
hummingbirds 187
hyenas 198

I

impalas 158, 182
insects 8, 14, 18, 20, 34-35, 50, 54-55, 58-59, 68, 71, 80-81, 98, 106-107, 114, 134, 139, 149, 152-153, 160-161, 162, 193, 198, 206, 209, 214-215, 218-219

J

jaguars 180
jawfish 207
jellyfish 6, 44, 175

K

kangaroos 10, 78, 86
Kea parrots 102
koalas 146

L

lambs 150-151
leeches 198
lions 128
lobsters 18, 172-173
locusts 34-35

M

mice 75, 142, 188
moles 125, 160
monkey grasshoppers 81
mosquitoes 162

N

netcasting spiders 85

O

octopuses 52-53, 61, 169, 177
orangutans 120
owls 132-133, 204-205, 210-211

P

Panamanian frogs 147
pandas 108-109
parrotfish 70-71
peacock mantis shrimp 31
penguins 122-123, 130
pigs 38, 193
poison dart frogs 11
polar bears 84, 125, 217
porcupines 199
prairie dogs 155

R

rabbits 32-33
rats 24-25, 213
red-billed oxpeckers 182
red shrimp 175
rhinoceroses 67
ribbon worms 114

S

sailfish 29
sardines 4-5
sea otters 159
sea urchins 94
seals 124
sharks 19, 29, 75, 111, 137, 164-165
sheep 22-23, 62-63
sloths 208
slugs 8
snails 23, 121, 131, 135
snakes 66, 99, 129
sperm whales 90-91, 200-201
spiders 37, 82-83, 85, 104-105, 206
spotted skunks 138
squirrels 86
starfish 36, 121
swallows 40-41

T

thorn bugs 58-59
tortoises 48, 161
turtles 8, 186-187, 202-203

W

walruses 149
whales 20, 90-91, 200-201, 216
wolf spiders 104-105
wolves 181
wombats 49

PHOTO CREDITS

COVER: WestEnd61/Rex Features, Gerard Lacz/Rex Features, © Eric Isselée/Fotolia.com

4-5 Steve De Nee/Solent News/Rex Features; **7** © Mammut Vision/Shutterstock.com; **8** (l) © Anteromite/Shutterstock.com (r) Michael S. Nolan/SplashdownDirect/Rex Features; **9** © Studio 37/Shutterstock.com; **10** © MaXPdia/iStock.com; **11** (c/r) © Alfredo Maiquez/iStock.com, (t) © ayzek/Shutterstock.com; **12** (sp) © Eric Isselée/Shutterstock.com, (c) © luchschen/iStock.com; **13** Wenn/SSPCA; **14** (t) © Bogdan Dumitru/Fotolia.com, (c) © Kirsty Pargeter/Shutterstock.com; **15** (b) © NatUlrich/Shutterstock.com, (t) Agencia EFE/Rex Features; **17** Barcroft Media via Getty Images; **18** (b) © Connie Wade/Fotolia.com, (t) © Kirsty Pargeter/Shutterstock.com; **19** © hxdbzxy/Shutterstock.com; **20** (b) © Birsen Cebeci/Shutterstock.com; **22** Ross Land/AP/Press Association Images; **23** AFP/Getty Images; **24** © Ivan Bliznetsov/iStock.com; **25** © Sergey Bolkin/Shutterstock.com; **26** Gavin Oliver/Solent News/Rex Features; **27** © (t/r) Eric Isselée/Shutterstock.com, (c/r) © Jo Lomark/Shuttetstock.com; **28** (l) © Ken Klotz/iStock.com, (r) © Andrey Kasimov/Shutterstock.com; **29** (b) © patrimonio designs limited/Shutterstock.com; **30** © Bernhard Richter/Shutterstock.com; **31** © cosma/Shutterstock.com; **32-33** (sp) Action Press/Rex Features; **33** (t) © Goncharuk/Shutterstock.com; **34-35** Reuters/Juan Medina; **36** © Darren Scanlin/Fotolia.com; **38** Barry Batchelor/PA Archive/Press Association Images; **39** NTI Media Ltd/Rex Features; **40-41** Keith Williams/Solent News/Rex Features; **42** (sp) © Slyers/Shutterstock.com, (t, b) © NHPA/ Joe Blossom; **45** (b) Adam Tinney/Shutterstock.com; **46-47** Albanpix Ltd/Rex Features; **48** Brad Hunter/Newspix/Rex Features; **51** © Justin Horrocks/iStock.com; **52-53** Bournemouth News/Rex Features; **54** © Anton Gvozdikov/Shutterstock.com; **55** © Faraways/Shutterstock.com; **56-57** www.sell-my-photo.co.uk; **58-59** © NHPA/Photoshot; **60** © Dan Lee/Shutterstock.com; **62-63** (sp) Carol McCabe/Rex Features; **63** (t) © Alexander Kaludov/Shutterstock.com; **64** Rex Features; **65** © NHPA/Photoshot; **66-67** © NHPA/Photoshot; **68-69** Wayne Davies/Rex Features; **70** © Stuart Westmorland/Corbis; **72-73** © Oceans Image/Photoshot; **74** Gerard Lacz/Rex Features; **75** © tristan tan/Shutterstock.com; **76-77** David Jones/PA Archive/Press Association Images; **78** © Thomas Amby/Shutterstock.com; **79** © NHPA/Photoshot; **80** Rundstedt Rovillos/Solent News/Rex Features; **81** (l) Caters; (r) © NHPA/Photoshot; **82-83** Reuters/Daniel Munoz; **84** © Andy Rouse/Naturepl.com; **85** © NHPA/Photoshot; **86** © Aaron Amat/Shutterstock.com; **87** Action Press/Rex Features; **88** Gavin Rodgers/Rex Features; **89** Reuters/Yuri Maltsev; **90-91** © NHPA/Photoshot; **93** Getty Images; **94** © Fabien Monteil/Shutterstock.com; **95** © AdShooter/iStock.com; **96** Jamie Hall/Solent News/Rex Features; **97** © Prill Medienesign und Fotografie/Shutterstock.com; **98** © Potapov Alexander/Shutterstock.com; **100-101** KeystoneUSA-Zuma/Rex Features; **102** Action Press/Rex Features; **103** (l) KPA/Zuma/Rex Features, (r) John O'Reilly/Rex Features; **104-105** © Bruce Coleman/Photoshot; **106** © Mixrinho/Shutterstock.com; **107** (t) © Thomas Amby/Shutterstock.com; **108-109** Reuters/China Daily China Daily Information Corp/CDIC; **110** Gerard Lacz/Rex Features; **111** © Rich Carey/Shutterstock.com; **112-113** Paul Lovelace/Rex Features; **116** © Wei-Chieh Wu/iStock.com; **117** NASA/Rex Features; **118-119** Newspix/Rex Features; **120** WestEnd61/Rex Features;

121 © myway2studio/Shutterstock.com; 122-123 © Solvin Zankl/Nature Picture Library; 126-127 Rex Features; 128 © Tetra Images/Photoshot; 129 © Alexander Lukin/Shutterstock.com; 131 Andrew Price/Rex Features; 132-133 BNPS.co.uk; 134 © Dmitry Naumov/iStock.com; 136 Michael Yang/Rex Features; 137 © pinare/Shutterstock.com; 138 © John Downer Productions/Naturepl.com; 139 Ciju Cherian/Solent News/Rex Features; 140-141 Israel Sun/Rex Features; 143 Image Broker/Rex Features; 144-145 © NHPA/Photoshot; 146 © Mark Higgins/iStock.com; 147 © Darren Green/Fotolia.com; 148 © Noluma/iStock.com; 149 © naluwan/Shutterstock.com; 150-151 Richard Austin/Rex Features; 152-153 Krista Queeney/Solent News/Rex Features; 154 © Jeryl Tan/iStock.com; 155 © Andrey Kuzmin/Fotolia.com; 156-157 © Norbert Wu/Minden Pictures/Corbis; 158 Frank Solomon/Solent/Rex Features; 159 © Andreas Mundorf/iStock.com; 160 © Arkady/Shutterstock.com; 161 © Alex Staroseltsev/Shutterstock.com; 163 © oksana2010/Shutterstock.com; 164 © Andrew Reid/Fotolia.com; 165 (t/r) © Eric Isselée/iStock.com, (t/l) © Ivan Bajic/iStock.com, (b/r) © Jodi Jacobson/iStock.com, (b/l) © MorePixels/iStock.com; 166-167 Dominik Schmies/Solent News/Rex Features; 169 © Michèle Tétrault/iStock.com; 172-173 © Doug Perrine/Naturepl.com; 174 © NHPA/Photoshot; 175 (l) © Ingo Amdt/Naturepl.com, (r) © David Shale/Naturepl.com; 177 © Ron van Elst/Shutterstock.com; 178-179 Mike Walker/Rex Features; 180 Ruth Savitz/Solent News/Rex Features; 182 Jochen Gerlach/Solent News/Rex Features; 183 (l) © Anatolii Tsekhmister/iStock.com, (r) © Marius Graf/iStock.com; 184 Paul Brown/Rex Features; 185 AFP/Getty Images; 186 Mike Roberts/Solent News/Rex Features; 188 © abrakadabra/Shutterstock.com; 189 © René Lorenz/iStock.com; 190 Rex Features; 192 © Thank You/Shutterstock.com; 193 © Goran J/Shutterstock.com; 194-195 Caters News Agency Ltd/Rex Features; 196 Greenpeace/Rex Features; 198 © szefei/Shutterstock.com; 199 © baseli01658/Shutterstock.com; 200-201 © Wild Wonders of Europe/Lundgren/Naturepl.com; 203 Chris Van Wyk; 204-205 Chris Balcombe/Rex Features; 206 Caters; 207 © Oceans Image/Photoshot; 208 © Alexander Rybakov/iStock.com; 209 © Hugh Lansdown/Shutterstock.com; 210 Henrik Nilsson/Solent News/Rex Features; 211 Dan Kitwood/Rex Features; 212 (l) Lewis Durham/Rex Features, (r) Stewart Cook/Rex Features; 214-215 Ingo Arndt/Nature Picture Library; 219 Wim Van Egmond/Visuals Unlimited, Inc./Science Photo Library.

Key: t = top, b = bottom, c = centre, l = left, r = right, sp = single page, dp = double page

All other photos are from Ripley Entertainment Inc. Every attempt has been made to acknowledge correctly and contact copyright holders and we apologise in advance for any unintentional errors or omissions, which will be corrected in future editions.

we hope you enjoyed the book!

If you have a fun fact or silly story, why not email us at bionresearch@ripleys.com or write to us at
BION Research, Ripley Entertainment Inc., 7576 Kingspointe Parkway, 188, Orlando, Florida 32819, U.S.A.